1964

C

REVOLUTION IN THE CITY

REVOLUTION IN THE CITY

Vincent J. Giese

With an Introduction by James V. Cunningham

FIDES PUBLISHERS, NOTRE DAME, INDIANA

By the Same Author: PATTERNS FOR TEENAGERS
TRAINING FOR LEADERSHIP

Library of Congress Catalog Card Number: 61-17711

CONTENTS

CONTENTS

INTRODUCTION

Man needed thousands of years to create the city, probably his most intricate and magnificent physical achievement.

Between the Neolithic village and the walls and towers of Ur, Babylon and Athens stood the sweat, scheming and applied wisdom of hundreds of generations. Even in modern America the development of a New York or Chicago has required a century.

Now in our era of turmoil and change whole sections of a city can be transformed and remade in a few brief years, in a mere fleeting moment as history is reckoned.

Sudden and radical changes, like the attack and pillage of old, have profound consequences for the men and women who inhabit cities and seek therein the good life.

And such changes have profound consequences for the cities themselves.

Pressures against a Troy or a Carthage were from without. Today's drastic changes result from pressures within the city, pressures of insecurity, racial antagonisms, crowding, obsolescence, unemployment.

The contemporary city is in a fight for survival.

In many ways it is failing to meet the challenge of change, failing to develop as a good place for human life. And the suburbs beyond offer an alternative, however feeble.

Much knowledge is needed and many actions must be taken if the city is to remain one of civilization's most useful tools.

Valuable and erudite studies of urban change have been made by sociologists and other probers and observers. These cooly objective studies have helped us know the components of change. They have assisted us in making plans to rebuild the city as a vital center of human life.

But these observers have not given us the full story.

One of the most significant changes flows from racial upheaval: the sudden displacement of the white population in a neighborhood by Negroes. Such changes have been particularly dramatic in the in-migration cities, those Northern metropolises like Detroit, Chicago and Cleveland which through job opportunities and the layout of rail lines have experienced prodigious increases in Negro move-ins during the past two decades.

In analyzing cases of such change the observers have told us much about the stages of change, the techniques of those who stimulate and those who seek to slow it. They have revealed for us such phenomena as the "tip point," the "self-fulfilling prophecy," and the exploitive real estate practices that accompany racial change.

But there is a need for something more. We need to see this upheaval also from the inside to understand it fully. We need subjective studies that bear the heat of panic and fear, the tragedy of flight and misunderstanding, the heroism of the courageous souls working against the tide. Insights are possible in such a story that the sociologists can never feel, know or relate.

This book is such a story.

We know from such a story that the task of creating the good city in our time is a frightening one. And we know, too, it is worth doing.

James V. Cunningham,
Action-Housing, Inc.,
Pittsburgh, Pa.
July 31, 1961

Forgive us, O Lord, the sins of our city.

Forgive us our sins of *pride*. Although our ancestors came from faraway lands to settle in our city, we have so soon forgotten our own humble origins. Our forefathers came with foreign tongues and foreign culture, awkward, unlettered, and gaudy of dress, but our city received them with open hearts and open arms. It gave them the start of a new way of life. Today we have become sophisticated. We have forgotten our past and hardened our hearts against newcomers in our midst.

Forgive us this pride, O Lord. Forgive us our sophistication, our subtle discriminations, our lack of sensitivity to those whose lot has not been as blessed as ours. Forgive us our sins of racial hatred, our barriers which we have erected between White and Negro.

What a terrible hurt we inflict on our urban neighbors whenever we reject them as being unworthy of our neighborliness, our friendship, our acceptance, our recognition, our kindness, our decency. Forgive us the wounds our pride inflicts on them when we panic at the thought of their coming, flee at the sight of them,

1

ir their nearness, as though some sort of plague struck our neighborhood.

ehind all our arguments about declining property ilues, miscegenation, and urban deterioration — which we so quickly ascribe to some sort of black magic — is our pride, our status-consciousness, our concern over what the Joneses will say, our fears of loss of prestige, our feelings of racial superiority. This, and not the color of a man's skin or his racial or national origin or the nature of his Credo, is the cause of our pride. Give us the courage to be honest.

Make us humble, O Lord. Make us little. Make us insignificant in your eyes. Clothe us in a humility that will smother all fears and set us free again to walk our city's streets in the knowledge that people — wherever we go — are people, and as people they deserve our trust, our friendship, and our welcome.

Forgive us the *anger* of our city, O Lord. Forgive us the sins of violence, of assault, of murder, of cold-blooded desecration of human life. We know that our cities are turbulent, bawdy, and congested, that they bring together people from all walks of life, all national origins, all racial inheritances, all economic strata — the cultured and the illiterate, the quiet, good people and the nervous, mentally deficient, the slum-dwellers and the comfortable suburbanites. We know the city becomes the melting pot of all kinds of people, and in this process incompatibility rules the day, tempers flare, reason is beclouded, and people are hurt. We expect no earthly paradise in our city.

We know that where people are congested there will be problems which result in violence and physical injury.

But we pray for all those who do violence to other men, for whatever reason. We ask you, O Lord, to soothe emotions, reduce tensions, and stay the hands of the angry. We ask you to open up hearts and help man realize the immense dignity of his fellow men. In place of our anger, let there be fraternal charity, condescension, deference.

Give our police force strength in numbers and strength of heart. Give our courts men of justice, who are stern in meting out disciplines yet mellow in their concern for broken men who deserve justice tempered with mercy. Give our city the agencies it needs to rehabilitate the angry. Give our lawmakers the vision to spread our population, ensure it decent housing, education, equal job opportunity and freedom of residence, so that some of the causes of social disorganization so productive of violence — especially among the young — can be eliminated. Give us a safe city, so that women and children may find contentment among us, free from fear and worry about their dignity.

Forgive us the *lust* of our city, O Lord. Forgive us the hustlers and procurers, forgive us the softness of life which too much of everything has given us and the hardness of heart which comes with softness of body. In our abundance, our ease, our luxury, our leisure, we lust after everything that is presented to our eyes. Panderers abound among us to tantalize our desires with every satisfaction of the human flesh. Forgive us the lines of prostitutes and sexual deviates who feed on sex-centered products of unscrupulous men living off of human weakness. Forgive us those whose business it is to purvey all kinds of smut through magazines, movies, advertisements, and cheap books in the glorification of the body as an object of desire.

Through our fault we have allowed these illicit enterpreneurs to thrive among us. Through our own moral weakness, our curiosity, our mediocrity, our insatiability, we have promoted their wares. In our hypocrisy we have too often castigated when we should have looked deep within our own moral consciousness to discover our own basic selfishness and disregard for the dignity of the body, particularly that of woman.

Give us a respect for womanhood. Give us a guarded, reserved, reticent respect for sex as a mystery which should be approached with modesty, purity, and chastity. Restore us to our innocence and make us slow to discover the mystery which you have wrapped in womanhood. Cover our eyes, stay our hands, calm our desires, curb our curiosity, and fill us with a love for the Virgin Mary, immaculate and undefiled.

Forgive us the *avarice* of our city, O Lord, as covetousness becomes the order of the day. Forgive us our real estate speculators who take advantage of innocent people in need of decent housing. Forgive us the mortgage bankers who discriminate in the use of money entrusted to them for the welfare of our community. Forgive us the loan sharks, the high interest rates, the usurious installment-buying plans, the swindlers who buy low and sell high, the hustlers who high-pressure their customers, who merchandise low quality at high prices, and who cause inflation.

Forgive us the cheaters, the bribers, the dishonest policemen, the payola. Forgive us the high costs of medicine and hospital care, the hedgers on income tax payment, the low minimum wages which we fail to raise by law. Forgive us the lobbyists, the special interest groups, the petty politicians, the traffic-court scandals, the short-changers, the market-manipulators and the price-riggers.

Forgive us our lack of concern in organizing white-collar workers into unions. Forgive us the wholesale robbers who operate under the cloak of respectable business, as well as the petty thieves and vandals, car-strippers and pickpockets and shoplifters. Dishonesty, whether on a large, organized respectable scale, or through petty personal crimes perpetrated by teen-agers, is rampant among us, and who shall cast the first stone? Firm up our sense of justice, O Lord, in the little things of everyday life.

Forgive us our *gluttony,* O Lord. Forgive us the alcoholics among us, those who have made a god of drink. Help them fill the emptiness of their lives — which they now fill with drink — with nobler goals, ideals, and dedication. Forgive them the harm they work against their family and friends and co-workers, the humiliations and heartbreaks they cause. Forgive them the sins they commit against their children, in

5

particular, who are being deprived of good example, moral leadership, and the love and respect they have a right to share with their parents.

But also forgive those among us, O Lord, who have grown flabby with food and drink, who have become diet-happy and weight-conscious, who have spent too much time and money taking off what gluttony has led us to put on. Give us that Spartan-like attitude towards the good things of life, so that we neither amuse or abuse ourselves in a way that deprives the needy of the minimum things of life.

Forgive us the waste in our lives, the overproduction and overconsumption which is done in the name of a healthy economy but which results in a flabby moral fibre. Keep us mindful of the poor, whom we always have with us and because of whom we may yet enter the Kingdom of Heaven.

Forgive us the *envy* of our city, O Lord. Let us look carefully beneath all the status symbols of our environment to see the envy and petty jealousies that underpin them. Forgive us the subtle rationalizations which motivate us to avoid this neighborhood or that neighbor, this house or that place of employment, this club or that social set, this kind of car or that kind of power-mower. In the deadening conformity that pushes us to structure ourselves in a certain class of society and adopt all its patterns, we lose all sense of communication with and openness to those below us. How much envy there is in our hearts which makes us feel superior to those beneath us and jealous of those above us.

Forgive us our struggle for acceptance and our fear of rejection, upon which envy feeds. Give us the clear vision to see through the false heroes and social goals which a phony commercialization has held before our eyes as standards of acceptability and arrival. Restore to us that delicate set of values which defines the good life, not in terms of consumer products, but in terms of contributions to the well-being of our fellow men, the only means by which true happiness on earth can be achieved.

Finally, O Lord, forgive us the *sloth* in our city. Forgive us our apathy, our laziness, our corroding self-contentment, our satisfaction with mediocrity, our preoccupation with the life of ease and leisure, our dullness, our tranquilized stupor, our inactivity in the face of overriding urban problems which call for vigorous and self-effacing action for a solution.

Forgive us our failure to vote, to take an interest in civic affairs and community associations. Forgive us our lack of social responsibility, our "Let George do it" attitude, our preoccupation with our own little self-enclosed world to the neglect of the world around us. Forgive us our political apathy, our civic apathy, and our spiritual apathy, our disdain for any effort which does not yield an economic profit or self-interest, or which requires self-sacrifice for the common good.

Give us the strength to leave our homes to take

part in the community around us, to attend meetings, to give leadership, to serve on committees, to
ring doorbells, to organize our neighbors, to sacrifice
our time and talent for the many voluntary associations — the strength of our democracy — which need
our help and our support. Give to our families an
understanding of this social role which all must play.
Give us the asceticism needed to venture forth in
these activities which are bound up so intimately today with the salvation of our city.

Remember the city, O Lord, and grant it salvation.

I
RACIAL CHANGE
IN A NEIGHBORHOOD

I moved into a stable, preferential neighborhood on the South Side of Chicago in 1952. I call it a preferential community because of its beautiful apartment buildings, proximity to fast transportation into Chicago's Loop area, excellent shopping facilities, ample schools, parks, playgrounds, churches, and many other social services. The area could be classified as a middle-income, predominantly rental area of choice urban living.

The past several years this community has undergone rapid racial change from an all-White to a predominantly Negro community.

What follows in these pages is a personal chronicle of one who has tried to remain calm and fearless amidst a vortex of change which literally has upended a community and socially disintegrated it.

I write these words out of a strong conviction that the problems involved in racially changing neighborhoods in our large urban centers are perhaps the most serious internal ones our nation faces today, the solution to which will have far-reaching effects on our national character. From the viewpoint of the Church — which is caught up in these changing times, just as so many other social institutions are — the social upheaval wrought in changing neighborhoods seriously threatens the moral fibre of her members and, in my own humble theological opinion, impedes

9

the flow of grace into their lives. Changing neighborhoods have forced the Church to redefine her mission in the urban center and make all kinds of new adaptations both in relation to her own parishioners and in relation to the community at large.

For sake of discussion, the broad community of which I write will be limited to the area which our parish embraces, which from the point of view of its 20,000 inhabitants, is a city in itself. From the central location of our parish church, the community is rather clearly divided between a pocket of single-family homes to the north and a densely populated modern apartment area to the south.

At the time when I moved into the community, the Negro in-migration had been advancing steadily but gradually southward from Chicago's Negro ghetto but it posed no immediate threat to our community, in that the residents were fairly strongly persuaded that certain natural boundaries — a cemetery to the north and a main avenue to the west — would keep Negroes from advancing farther. Since the people believed this, there was not too much concern about approaching change. For example, an Improvement Association was organized to keep a careful eye on the Negro in-migration, and while a hard core of members were faithful and vigilant, the association was unable to enlist broad community support. Except among a few property owners, who feared the coming of the Negro would destroy property values, little enthusiasm was generated. The association busied itself with general community improvement projects, such as street lighting, commuter-train rates, sewers, garbage collection, etc., as it prepared itself for the advent of the Negro. In all honesty, it must be admitted that the main objective of the Improvement Association was to keep the Negro out. Money was available to enable the association to buy property, if necessary, to achieve this end.

In 1955 our parish was at full strength. It was a thriving, healthy parish of some eight thousand Catholics and 650 elementary school students. The parish physical plant consisted of a modern church and school, a rectory and a convent, and a full complement of teaching Sisters. It had grown tremendously the past twenty years from an Italian immigrant mission church to a fully developed territorial parish of all nationalities and incomes — a typical urban parish in America. And it was out of debt.

In 1956 racial change took place in the northern corner of the parish at the juncture of the so-called natural boundaries — the cemetery and the avenue — but it happened almost unnoticed by the general populace and it was still a mile away from the huge apartment-building area. Racial change was in the air, however, for the parish west of us had been undergoing change, and the Negroes were on the move into the fringe neighborhoods touching on the southern and western boundaries of the Negro ghetto. By 1956 Negroes had already moved solidly along the western boundary of our parish, separated from us only by the main avenue of Cottage Grove.

11

Apart from the growing number of Negroes at busy intersections, one of the first signs of change was the gradual emptying out of the commercial area along Cottage Grove. As to be expected, one vacancy after another appeared, as White shopkeepers, faced with a change of clientele, moved quickly to new areas where they could preserve the all-White character of their businesses. Then, too, most of these small businesses were of such marginal character that they could not withstand the loss of business which change necessarily brought. Except for certain types of business, where the racial character of the clientele makes little difference, clothing and apparel shops, shoe stores, barbershops, doctors, dentists, bakeries were quick to move. Cottage Grove and some of the commercial streets which had been so alive before now became like ghost towns. Real estate dealers were about the only new store-front occupants to rush in.

The shopping area, so important to the residents of a community, was now in an interim period. Not enough Negroes were in the area yet to justify Negro merchants moving in, and not enough Whites were left to make it profitable for the White merchants to operate. Obviously, as the commercial nature of an urban area deteriorates and small businesses flee, one of the attractive features of urban living is lost — really a first sign of neighborhood deterioration, and one which can be a major factor, in itself, why people would begin thinking of moving out of the community.

Among the stores that remained, groceries, chains and drugstores were fairly integrated at the customer level, particularly the grocery stores, which had long served Negro customers. Middle-class Negroes had traditionally gone out into White neighborhoods to buy groceries, especially meats, because they felt they could buy better foods in those neighborhoods than in their own communities.

With these beginning evidences of change, it was obvious in late 1956 that the community would soon begin to receive Negroes in large numbers. Negro faces were in sufficient evidence in the community for property owners to push the panic button, and, of course, the horde of fly-by-night real estate dealers moved into the area, hung out shingles, and prepared for the big financial kill opening up to them in a panicky area. The button had been pushed. The climate in this once staid and stable community was beginning to change. The coming of the Negro became the major topic of conversation, rumor, and concern.

Since our parish is divided rather distinctly into two areas — the single-family, open residential area to the north (Grand Crossing) and the huge apartment area to the south (Chatham), I will consider these two communities separately.

Grand Crossing

The racial change in Grand Crossing was slow, for

most of these homes were owner-occupied by people of a lower income, many of whom could not afford to move. These people had lived in the community a long time and had worked hard to buy their homes; they had raised their families here, and many, at last, were enjoying old age and retirement. There were many family ties in the community, which was rather tightly-knit, full of traditions and community pride. Although change has been taking place in Grand Crossing for four years, still there has not been a complete changeover to a Negro community, but the ratio is now tipped in favor of the Negro. Blocks in some instances are still integrated at about a 50-50 ratio. In one section of Grand Crossing no change has taken place at all, as a tightly-knit Italian-American section of several blocks continues to hold together.

In my own block the ratio is 50-50, but interestingly enough little change has taken place in more than a year, except that five new brick homes have been built on vacant land and sold to Negroes. (That won't hurt our property values any.) Those who found it profitable have sold and moved; the rest will most likely hang on, at least for awhile, either because of financial hardships, old age, or simply because of a decision to make a go of interracial living and avoid all the headaches of pulling stakes and moving. Once people have lived in an integrated block for a year or so, their fears seem to calm down and they discover it isn't so terrible after all, so why fight it, why get all worked up, panic, and move. I must add that since these people are of a lower income level (steel-workers, tradesmen, truck drivers, civil service employees, maintenance men, etc.), the status problem of living next to Negroes doesn't mean as much to them as it does to professional or middle-class people. They are fairly democratic about it all.

One of my neighbors expressed the matter well to me. After an initial panic phase, then finding himself surrounded by Negroes, he said, "So far, so good." In other words, he had found his new neighbors acceptable. No great curse had come upon his house. Life was going on pretty much as before. He was sustained by the fact that some ten other White families on the block were staying. He wasn't alone. So he has made his decision to stay. In the twilight of life, with his family grown and his life's investment tied up in his house, as a factory worker and a good church member, he has no desire or financial resources to move to the suburbs. At the moment he seems satisfied that everything is going to work out all right. It is my guess that in this relaxed outlook, he may have added several years to his life. Unless the block continues to change, to a point where his is the last White family on the street, I believe he will stay.

When Grand Crossing began to change, real estate sharks went door to door to see if any of us wanted to sell our homes. Such remarks as the following were standard: "They are only a couple of blocks away, so you better sell now while you can get your price," or "You know, of course, that Mr. So-and-So just sold his home down the street." The general harassment contributed in no small degree to the panic atmosphere in the neighborhood. In some instances, the real estate speculators were more brazen than this in their block-busting attempts.

In this adventure of making quick deals by capitalizing on the fears of the people, all kinds of techniques are used. White real estate operators hire Negro people to sit on the front porch of a vacant home, to give the impression that Negroes have moved in. Telephone calls, wrong numbers, calls in the middle of the night (with voices of Negroes on the other end), a general harassment by phone and door bell and through the mails — all these techniques are common when a neighborhood begins to change, as an all-out attempt is made to bust a block open. Once the block can be busted, that is, the first house is sold to Negroes, then the real estate dealers have easy picking in moving up and down the block. The harassment itself is cause enough for some people to sell out; they just want to get away from it all and find some peace of mind.

In the real estate operations in a changing neighborhood, there is no discrimination. Both Negro and White operators are busy in the field, and both will employ Negro and White salesmen in order to be able to deal with all possible situations. The larger real estate agencies and management companies do not seem too interested in single-family units, admittedly because there is not enough money in the sale of these homes. They are interested in buying and selling big apartment buildings.

That leaves the single-family areas, such as Grand Crossing, open to the small, greedy operators. By scare tactics they are able to buy these homes at low prices, then turn around and sell them high on contract basis to Negroes desperate for housing. This kind of sale means a low down-payment but high monthly payments at high interest, with little protection in the event a payment is missed. The profits in these operations are fantastic, as some of these homes are sold two and three times over. The technique is to advertise them in the Negro newspapers. I know a man with a large family who bought a frame house, with a small income-paying garage apartment in the rear. When the recession hit and he was laid off, he fell behind in his payments and was issued a court order. He was also paying regularly on a second mortgage. Had not a Christian real estate dealer in our parish taken a personal interest in this case (he eventually loaned the man money out of his own pocket to make up his payments) the man would have been financially broken. The tragic part is that even if he is able to survive this crisis, he will be unable for years to put many improvements into his fifty-year old frame house. It is gradually deteriorating away. This is what creates slum conditions and lowers community standards.

17

In a block which begins to change, suspicion begins to spread among neighbors. Outwardly, the same community spirit of neighborliness prevails, and as neighbors meet and discuss on the streets, or as housewives meet at local stores, almost everyone says he intends to stay, not to panic and sell. "I will not be the first to sell, but I won't be the last, either," about sums up the attitude.

Inwardly, everyone is thinking about selling, because enough real estate men have gotten their feet in the door to provoke thought on the possibilities. Families begin to take council at the dinner table, pros and cons are weighed, rumors are bandied about as fact. It doesn't take too long for enough rationalization to set in to make selling or moving appear as the only practical course of action.

The attitudes crystallize. "I don't want to be the last one on the block to sell, or I'll never get my money back." Or, "I won't be the first to sell, but if someone else sells I'll be forced to do so." Or, "Property values will go down when the first Negro moves in." Many of these attitudes are placed in the people's minds by the real estate dealers who carry their message of unrest from door to door, exchange gossip, report information on what other neighbors are planning, etc.

The breakdown of mutual trust and neighborliness is inevitable, and then, when a block actually begins to change, another strange phenomenon takes place. The remaining White people on the block band together, become more chummy, as they form almost unconsciously their own little self-protection association, a ghetto-like haven of security. Eventually, of course, after the first exodus, the situation levels off, with fewer moves and more time between them. The block settles into a status quo. The real estate dealers have moved on to another block or another neighborhood, the pressure is off, and normalcy returns. But it may require several years for this metamorphosis to take place.

The newcomers, meanwhile, fit into the neighborhood pattern. Since this is the first opportunity for almost all of them to live in a home of their own, to own some personal property, to escape dense tenement areas of the Black Belt, they take to the new experience in urban living with zest and pride. They work in their yards, paint and fix up their homes. Their children mix freely with the few remaining White children, and seemingly without any parental objection on either side. Economically and occupationally, the newcomers are about on a par with their neighbors. Educationally, the newcomers may have the edge on the people they replaced; the families tend to be younger and larger than the ones which have remained. Due to a lack of equal job opportunities, the Negroes are probably not engaged in work equal to their capabilities and training, and certainly their job security is less, in event of an economic recession, a strike, a layoff. Then, too, to meet the high monthly payments on the homes, they may be required to double up, make room for another wage earner in the home who can help out financially and also help finance necessary remodeling and maintenance.

At present Grand Crossing is over the hump as far as change is concerned. Certainly, there will be more transition, but at a slower pace, for the mass exodus is a thing of the past. As far as the speculators are concerned, the bloom is off the flower. This does not mean Grand Crossing is now a peacefully integrated community, that interracial living has been achieved, that all problems are solved. It means that some sort of normal conditions prevail again as far as housing is concerned.

Chatham

Looking to the south part of our parish community, which I shall refer to as Chatham, a completely different pattern of racial change is evident. In this half square mile, the single family dwellings can be counted on two hands, whereas apartment buildings, from two and three flats to buildings containing up to a hundred units, exist side by side in an almost monotonous architectural frequency, with a certain majestic beauty highlighted by tall trees and small but well-kept lawns. The contrast between Grand Crossing and Chatham is striking, but the two areas are tied together by churches, shopping centers, schools, and public parks.

When change occurred slowly but relentlessly in Grand Crossing, the middle-class people living in

Chatham barely took notice. Grand Crossing seemed to be such a totally different type of community that the people were inclined to dismiss it, or at least to feel certain that a similar change couldn't happen in Chatham. Wiser heads, experienced in community work, had long predicted that when change would come to Chatham, which is heavily rental, it would come as a thief in the night and take place rapidly and totally. The very nature of the area made this inevitable, for the buildings themselves often were not owned by the people living in them but by outside investors — through anonymous trust funds — who had turned their property over to real estate management firms. The owners had absolutely no stake in the community except a financial one.

Unlike the homeowners in Grand Crossing, the apartment renters had no real stake in the community. They rented. They were commuters, settled here because of the excellent and quick transportation to their jobs in downtown Chicago, but without any financial interest in the area, and thus very little community responsibility. This is not to say these people did not have a warm spot in their hearts for the area — many had lived here twenty and twenty-five years. They were stable, middle-class people and, incidentally, they were the financial backbone of our parish and school. But, except for those who owned two and three flats, the people were not property-owners.

When the first Negroes moved into Chatham, the panic button was pushed. Renters who felt strongly about living in a community with Negroes had no qualms about leaving. When their leases expired, they moved. Owners of the smaller apartment buildings were quick to place them on the market and found them easy to sell and at good prices, for the Negro middle-class market was ready to buy at almost any price in order to break away from the ghetto and begin renting in what had always been considered one of Chicago's choicest communities.

Within a year and a half, the change in the area was fantastic. The managers of the large apartment buildings were willing to go along for a year with a few vacancies, in the hopes that White families could be induced to come into the area to take advantage of the transportation and other community services. But when it became difficult to fill these vacancies, the owners sold the buildings to Negroes (or began renting flats to Negroes) and thus by a changeover were able to fill the vacancies without difficulty and at an increased rental charge. Some buildings have remained interracial, but an increase in rent, proposed to the remaining White families, usually is the final straw in forcing people to leave, even though many of them might have otherwise stayed on.

Each spring and fall, when leases expire, a mass exodus has taken place. Many of the remaining White tenants are on a month-to-month lease, which means they can pull stakes, or be asked to leave, at whatever time they want to leave or the owner wants to make the building all-Negro.

If integration is still possible in Grand Crossing, if the change there has been gradual, and if the bloom is off the real estate market there, not so in Chatham. The rate of turnover has been fast, and few doubt that it will be all but complete. Not enough time has passed to allow for interracial living to set in.

Not all the reasons for moving have been economic, of course, even though it is true that the White people often had no choice but to move as buildings were sold or rented out from under them. In this densely populated apartment area, many other social and psychological factors were operative in the decision to move.

Whether founded in fact or not, fears of women and of the parents of young girls were a major cause of the decision to move. In large apartment buildings, where people can come and go with relative anonymity, where passageways are devious, and where conditions are favorable to prowlers, peeping Toms, purse-snatchers, dope addicts, and other petty criminals, women naturally are afraid, especially given their conviction that the crime rate is higher among Negroes than among Whites. It seems that enough petty crimes, perpetrated by Negroes — seldom by those living in the area but by outsiders who prey on changing communities — took place during the panic period to raise all kinds of fears, even among the most open-minded.

In an atmosphere of fear, double locks are placed on doors, older women literally become recluses for enturing out alone, watch dogs are bought, и and children are afraid to go on the streets after dark. Such a state of fear gripped the people of Chatham and cast an ominous psychological gloom over what was once an easygoing, carefree community. No one will ever be able to document just how much this fear was the figment of horrible imaginings of half-neurotic women, or how much of it had justification in fact, or how much of it was spawned on rumor and the techniques of ruthless real estate speculators. But the truth of the situation cannot be denied, and police statistics from the local police district indicate an increase in the crime rate in the area. The fact remains, Chatham has been gripped by fear, much more so than Grand Crossing. No husband and no family man can long withstand the fears of his womenfolks. He simply packs up his family and moves.

Perhaps the really tragic part of the entire transition is the fact that a stable community has been completely uprooted and disorganized — and largely by factors outside the personal control of the people involved. No matter how strongly one believes in the rights of Negroes to decent housing, the mass exodus of an entire community, literally overnight, is tragic, all the more so when most of the people were forced to move whether they wanted to or not. Many of these people had lived here some twenty years, all of their married life. They had raised their families in this community; they were solid church-goers; they had deep friendships and close associations in the community.

Had the decision to move been completely in the hands of the residents, one would not feel as badly about the consequences. But here is a situation where one community becomes inundated by Negroes who quite naturally are in search of housing in one of the few areas in Chicagoland open to them. The fault cannot be placed on the Negroes. Neither are the residents of the community to be blamed for the upheaval. Real estate speculators, absentee-landlords (hiding behind trusts), mortgage bankers, petty criminals from outside the area, building managers who unjustifiably raised rents — and society at large for closing off other parts of Chicago to Negroes — combined to create an almost impossible situation for the long-time residents to cope with. That such a situation could develop — and is developing over and over again — calls for a serious examination of the urban problem.

Running through it all, of course, is racial prejudice, not only among the residents of the community but among those of all of Chicago and its suburbs. It just so happens that racial prejudice has come to a nasty climax in our small community at this time; next year it will infect another neighborhood; and so it seemingly spreads from neighborhood to neighborhood, as a kind of grass fire. Where it will stop, or if it can be stopped at all, no one knows. Perhaps it is a new kind of Chicago fire that ultimately will destroy the city.

II

IN THE WAKE OF CHANGE

Despite the fact that racial change in Grand Crossing and Chathan has now nearly run its course, enormous new social problems have been created in the process. Solutions to these problems involving schools, youth programs, community organizations, political structures, churches and other community institutions must now be worked out in the community. Everything within the old community has been completely uprooted and a whole new population awaits social organization. In this chapter I would like to identify some of the major concerns of the community at this time.

The School Problem

Two of the public elementary schools in our community are already on double shifts. The school in the Grand Crossing area is already more than ninety per cent Negro, which indicates that most of the White families with school-age children have moved away, the fact that these people did not want their children to attend an interracial school being no small reason why they moved. The fear exists in the minds of most people in our community that a school in which Negroes are the majority will be an inferior school, that standards will necessarily be lowered, partly be-

cause of overcrowding, partly because the bett
teachers will move to schools in better neighborhood.

There is also the fear on the part of Whites of having their seventh- and eighth-grade children mingle
socially with Negro children of the same age. Once
sex differences are apparent and the children recognize
them, the parents no longer want their children to associate with Negro children. While they may have no
objection — but no enthusiasm, either — at the pre-
school age or during early years of grammar school
when sex attraction is no problem, their attitude now
changes. As one mother in our community explained
it to me, she is perfectly willing to live in an integrated
community, but now that her daughter is ready for
high school, has she, as a mother, the parental right
to keep her daughter in a predominantly Negro high
school? Is it the best thing for her daughter? Added
to this, she is a little uneasy when her daughter is
walked home from school each night by a half dozen
Negro boys.

In the public high school in our community, which
is now heavily Negro, very little integration has taken
place, except on the athletic fields. Otherwise, a kind
of peaceful coexistence would be the best way to describe relationships. White and Negro teenagers, except in a few isolated instances, have little communication. This is obvious even to an outsider walking
through the neighborhood in the vicinity of the school.
The Negroes and Whites keep pretty much to themselves, and from what the young people tell me, there

27

are some rather marked cultural differences between the two groups — something beyond color — which make integration difficult. Even in the matter of dress, it can be noted that all the Negro boys wear hats; not so the White boys. The Negro teenager tends more to the Ivy or Continental look in clothes, complete with umbrella, whereas the White boys wear wash pants and jackets. Those cultural differences extend to other areas such as language (teenage jargon), music, style of dance, and even choice of sports.

In our high school, many of the Negro teenagers come from a higher income group, from middle-class Negro families, many of whom live in an adjoining neighborhood which is somewhat comparable to a White suburban neighborhood. The few remaining White teenagers in our public school seem to be from blue-collar families. If anything, I am inclined to believe that the academic standards are improving rather than declining in our public high school, mainly because the school is not yet overcrowded. I also believe that the principal and his staff, conscious of the lower standards charge, are working diligently to maintain and to raise standards. Be that as it may, those who were most worried about standards have long since moved out of the area or have transferred their children to private high schools.

White students who might have cultivated some friends among their Negro classmates are aware that the friendships cannot extend much beyond the walls of the school. The problem of bringing their Negro friends into their homes is still a sensitive one. As the principal of the high school has correctly stated, no matter how conscientiously he and his staff may work for good human relations, in the final analysis the relations in the school will be no better or no worse than the general race relations that exist in the community.

Youth Facilities

In the center of the Grand Crossing area, facing our parish church and adjacent to the public high school, lies Grand Crossing Park. In addition to softball and baseball diamonds, tennis courts, play lots, and an outdoor swimming pool, there is a large fieldhouse with full indoor athletic facilities and meeting rooms. Needless to say, when and how to integrate activities in the park posed a very difficult community problem. From a legal point of view, a city ordinance leaves no doubt in anyone's mind that the park is for everyone, regardless of color, creed, race, or national origin. It is against the law for the authorities in charge of the park to discriminate against anyone in making the facilities available. An offended person could bring legal action against the city for any violation of the ordinance.

But as we well know from social situations, the law does not operate in a vacuum. In the case of the park, there is a set of traditional values which must be taken into consideration. Apart from the law, integration of the park means playing with a certain amount of dynamite.

29

Unfortunately, the White teenagers who have occupied the park since their boyhood are not possessed of all the complex sociological reasons behind discrimination, the subtleties of the law, the Christian values which should prevail, the democratic principles involved, or dedication to a cause. Very simply and bluntly, the whole complexus was reduced to a simple formula: "Keep the niggers out." In their immature minds, the park was the place to draw the battle line. During the summer the past few years, we simply drew a breath and prayed that no major race riot would break out.

A few minor skirmishes have taken place, provoked by roaming carloads of teenagers, White and Negro; a few garages have been set on fire; a few kids have been beaten up; a few sticks of dynamite have gone off in the park; gun-shot has been used; but terrible as all this might sound, the major race riot which could spread through South Chicago even to Gary, Indiana, has not been touched off. Fortunately, the police have been on the alert, various city agencies have kept a vigilant eye on the area, and some excellent juvenile work has been done in the park to keep things under control. As a matter of fact, at present the park has rather successfully passed the crisis.

Integration took place in Grand Crossing Park, first of all, and as long as three years ago, on the tennis courts and in the kiddie play lot. Tennis being an individual, not a group sport, and kiddies, accompanied by their parents as they slosh around in wading pools or use swings and slides, pose no serious threats. Next in line, and only the past year, came the softball and baseball diamonds, followed by the swimming pool, and finally, and last of all, the indoor activities inside the fieldhouse.

On the credit side, the remaining White teenagers seem to have given up some ground as time goes on, after several unsuccessful summers of battling with Negro youth. Perhaps they have grown a little older and more mature, but it is not uncommon to hear them concede now that the cause is lost, that battle is not worth the risks of jail, injury, police harassment, or that it is too late to save the neighborhood, so why fight it. If the White teenagers have been neutralized to this extent, perhaps the crisis period is past. Add to this the fact that the Negroes now outnumber the Whites. The White teenagers now find themselves in the minority position, and as a result they may now be in for trouble.

Community Organization

A third problem lies in the area of community organization against the corroding effects of illegal conversion, overcrowding, blight, crime rates, inadequate parking facilities, and all the other factors which contribute to neighborhood deterioration, particularly in an area such as Grand Crossing with its forty-year-old frame houses. To fight against these neighborhood evils, community organization is needed to educate the people, build community morale, and

31

tap the various city agencies and services, commissions and departments for help in conforming the area to city housing, zoning, fire, and health codes.

The kind of community action called for must be representative of all the people living in the area. Leadership must be found and encouraged and developed among the newcomers as well as among those who have remained. Broad-based community action and local block clubs must be organized in a positive effort on the part of the people to live and work successfully together to maintain a good, healthy community. In such changing communities, often the only organizations in existence are those whose pattern in the past has been to keep the neighborhood all-White.

Under such conditions, the incoming Negroes certainly would not feel welcome, nor would they be — even the more responsible among them who are sincerely interested in community standards. Either these existing organizations must undergo a change in leadership and policy — in line with the new structure of the community — or new community associations must be formed on the premise that the neighborhood has changed and, therefore, what can be done now to preserve it, conserve it, integrate it, stabilize it, and keep it from becoming just another in a string of contiguous all-Negro ghettos eating away at our inner cities.

In Grand Crossing-Chatham, an Improvement Association, which had functioned eight or more years under a "keep them out" policy was finally and painfully retooled by a new leadership which accepted the real situation and recognized the simple fact that unless a community association is representative of the people, it will be useless and powerless. After a year, it has become fully integrated, and its programs and activities have proved to be a heart-warming experience in democracy and a vote of confidence in the future.

Politics

A fourth problem lies in the area of politics. The political implications of a changing neighborhood are far-reaching in terms of over-all city planning and development. On the one hand, the incumbent political leaders hope to bring the newcomers under their political tents, keep them happy, but still retain political control of the area. Nothing is more disconcerting to an incumbent than to see his constituency constantly changing. On the other hand, some of the more politically ambitious Negro leaders hope to swing the balance of political power to the side of the Negro, so that still another political area can be placed under Negro political control. There are those who operate on the principle, right or wrong, that the only way the Negro will attain his full rights in Chicago lies in political control of City Hall, so that necessary legislation to guarantee Negro equality can be enacted.

Whichever political approach ultimately prevails,

it is certain that political leaders at the ward level in our large cities today will have to build their campaigns and programs on questions of urban renewal, redevelopment, neighborhood conservation, transportation, educational facilities, and so on, for these are the issues uppermost in the mind of the citizen today. The need for enlightened ward politicians — even precinct captains — who will cooperate with local community associations is obvious today. The political leaders of tomorrow in local areas, and perhaps nationally, will be those men who have a vision of urban problems as they beset our large cities. This, perhaps more than anything else, will redefine political parties and platforms in the future. Taxes, welfare agencies, transportation, civil rights, housing, the relation of suburbs to the city, the exploding metropolis, "urban sprawl" — all these concrete problems ultimately are political issues.

Furthermore, I believe that our local political leaders of the future are now being trained in voluntary community associations. The growth and multiplication of high-minded community organizations on the southeast side of Chicago is amazing. Out of these organizations are coming pressures on City Hall on matters such as rezoning, enforcement of housing and building codes, improved city services. Citizens no longer contact their precinct captains or aldermen for action in these areas. They go to their block club captains and to their community associations, which in turn, as organizations, bring pressure for action on the alderman and the city agencies. Results are usually forthcoming. In my opinion, the alderman is becoming less of a political or civic leader today; he is a kind of broker between the community association and City Hall. And he had better cooperate, or he will not long stay in office.

I was amused when I attended a meeting of our alderman's Legislative Advisory Committee — a committee he very wisely established to afford him the opportunity to meet regularly with representatives of all the various community and civic associations in his ward. Speaking facetiously, but perhaps with more truth than he would care to admit, he said about the only thing he could do well any more in our community was to remove abandoned cars. He conceded that the community associations were handling everything else.

If this trend continues, and I see no reason why it won't, we may soon see the day when the whole concept of ward organization of a city will be obsolete. Even at the grass-roots level, the block club captains are the power men today, not the precinct captains, whom most of the people see only at election time. The block captains, elected by the people, meet regularly with the people of their block to tend to housekeeping chores on the block. These block clubs in turn are part of a larger community association which can bring the collective strength of the community to bear if and when a particular block needs action.

35

I had an opportunity not too long ago to sit in on a block club meeting among some of the new residents. The meeting was held at one of the local churches, whose minister had been hosting various block clubs in an effort to bring the people together (and incidentally, in the hope some would come back to services on Sunday). I was impressed by the high level of community interest among the ten or so Negroes present. Middle-class, articulate, mature, responsible, these people had a deep interest in preserving community standards.

One woman was disturbed that some of the basements on her block might be illegally converted into apartments. She was fearful of overcrowding. Another was alarmed that a large apartment building had been sold to Negroes with families. She was afraid too many children in the building would deteriorate it. Another young Negro came to the meeting because he wanted to do something in providing athletic facilities for the boys in his block. A real estate operator expressed a keen interest in joining the association to work for conservation of the area. And so the discussion continued. I left the meeting with the conviction that a high-type of Negro had moved in among us, and that the newcomers were ready to take a leadership role in the community. They were enthusiastic about forming a block club. Hardly a week goes by that our community association is not called upon to assist in the formation of a new block club.

Churches

A final problem posed in a changing neighborhood involves our Churches. While all denominations face a period of readjustment — as long-time parishioners move away from the community and new ones must be found to replace them — I would like to discuss the role of the Catholic Church in my community. In a not untypical situation, our neighborhood had some eight thousand Catholics at its peak year in 1958, all of whom were counted as members of our parish. Today we have some 1500 adult Catholics, in addition to several hundred school children. The exodus is not yet completed.

At the high point of its history, during the 1950's, our parish priests concentrated their efforts on servicing the large number of Catholics in the area. A full parish plant was built and paid for and staffed with priests and teaching Sisters. Traditional organizations flourished, with a gradual development of specialized forms of Catholic Action — the Christian Family Movement, the Young Christian Workers, the Young Christian Students, and the Confraternity of Christian Doctrine. The life of the parish was healthy and vigorous.

As racial change took place, it was obvious the parish would enter into a new period of its history, marked by a falloff in membership, as well as income, since the newcomers to the area were not Catholic, except for the usual estimated six per cent characteristic of the Negro population.

37

Several new problems were immediately posed to the priests of the parish. One, the need to shift to a missionary operation, with an aggressive convert-making program for the new arrivals. Two, an attempt had to be made to hold as many White parishioners as possible to preserve some kind of integrated parish. Both problems required redefinition of goals for the parish in place of the traditional conserve-the-faith approach.

The priests, first of all, had to take an interest in the change going on in the area, which meant taking an interest in neighborhood conservation, housing, community standards, zoning, enforcement of city codes, all of which are aimed at keeping the community stable and healthy. Not only the priests, but lay leaders from the parish had to be involved in the work of the community association.

Actually, all the Churches — led by their ministers — were of one mind in these matters. Community association meetings became something of an ecumenical meeting, with as many as six or eight ministers attending a given meeting, and for the first time getting to meet and know one another and join together in common work at neighborhood improvement.

On the parish level, traditional parish societies naturally dwindled in membership and vitality, and even the specialized movements declined, as the YCW and YCS eventually folded up for lack of stable membership. Only the Christian Family Movement has survived, now healthier than ever, and in fact is now an integrated group.

In the analysis of the priests, the time was particularly ripe for convert-winning programs, and whereas only a handful would join an inquiry class during the prime years of the parish, this fall more than one hundred were signed up for instructions. On the conviction that many of the Negroes, particularly the men, were not yet religiously committed to any denomination, an intensive promotion campaign to find prospects was launched, complete with home-visiting on the part of a team of men lined up for the work. The results are evident.

Opening up the Catholic school to non-Catholic children, on condition that the parents take an inquiry course, helped bring the school back to near-capacity, and in the long run will yield results in the convert field. The long, hard job of rebuilding a new parish with new parishioners is underway.

Phase two is concerned with revitalizing and reorganizing the traditional parish societies. Negroes must be brought into these, given status, accepted, and given programs within broad-based organizations, so that they come to feel a vital part of parish life. This is particularly essential for converts, who simply cannot be baptized, then abandoned to shift on their own. They need to be picked up and identified with parish life, so that their religious knowledge will have an opportunity to grow and deepen at a time when they are most eager and zealous in their new beliefs.

Phase three is liturgical — a gradual introduction of dialogue and sung Masses, again so the new Catholic catches some of the community spirit and can participate in the worship life of the parish.

In short (and I will treat each of these matters at greater length in later chapters), integration of parish organizations, discovery of new leadership material, broad-based programming that will appeal to all the people, a well-organized CCD program of religious instruction, and participation in the liturgy — these are immediate pastoral goals which must be implemented in a parish in a changing neighborhood. Not to mention the tremendous task of bringing the parish back economically, for it cannot continue to live on savings or diocesan help. These are all problems that call for vigorous and imaginative action on the part of pastor and assistants and for all the help of the laity that can be mobilized.

One factor must always be borne in mind. The church, more particularly the Catholic Church, is a powerful institution in a racially changing community. It has a vested interest, it has prestige and status, it has power, it has priests who hold high positions of esteem in the community. In the final analysis, it may be the most powerful institution in the community.

With this favored position come both rights and responsibilities. The Church has a responsibility to take a strong role in community action. It has this responsibility to its people, its property investment,

40

and to the community as a whole. The Church will play no small part in the success or failure of the social reorganization and stabilization of the new community taking shape. How it exercises these responsibilities, whether or not it acts selfishly as a power group, as a vested-interest group, or whether it keeps an open mind to the common welfare of the community at large becomes the all-important question. The Church must never use community organizations for its own ends, for example, or use its favored position to run roughshod over other religious denominations not quite so strong, or act politically in any way that might be interpreted wrongly in the public mind.

Always the Church must be aware that it is in a pluralistic situation in a community. Perhaps there is no greater self-protective step that it can take in offsetting the temptation to flaunt its power and position than to act through its lay leaders rather than through its priests. Lay leaders will have a more balanced outlook on the common good of the community and from the perspective of the resident, while still retaining a balanced image of the Church. The great danger of clericalism in community organization work can be offset by careful selection of lay leaders to join in this work with the full support of the Church and its priests. While we have safely outgrown the age of *labor priests,* perhaps we must now be careful of an age of *community priests.* Wherever priests can find laymen to carry the lead, I believe they should themselves stay in the background.

Conclusion

A new community is taking shape. New leaders will emerge. New community associations will develop. Churches will take in new members. The old community is gone. The White people are dispersed. The really disheartening thing about it all is that the new community taking place will probably not be very integrated. It will be almost all Negro, just as the old community was all White.

III

YOUTH IN A
CHANGING NEIGHBORHOOD

It was an early summer evening when I strolled across the park to see what was going on among the young people. Half way across I noticed a little scuffling among some young White and Negro boys. At the same time I crossed paths with two older White boys whom I knew well in the neighborhood. They were headed for the swimming pool for their evening dip. I stopped my friends, pointed to the action in the far corner and suggested they walk over with me to break up the fight. The suggestion, to say the least, did not inspire them. As we began our slow walk to the scene of action, the boys kept trying to wiggle out of their assignment. I kept needling them about their leadership abilities. As we approached, a group of white boys had two Negro boys surrounded. It didn't look too promising. In a last desperate attempt to avoid the encounter, one of my friends pleaded. "Look, you do it this time, and we will watch, to see how you handle it." I wasn't impressed.

Finally, my friend moved into the situation. "What's going on here?" he asked. The reply came. "These Niggers are playing in the park." My friend fired back in a strong clear voice, "What's it to you? Come

on. Let's go swimming. Leave those guys alone."
With that the White boys followed him sullenly to
the pool.

This small incident happened several years ago when
the racial change first began in my neighborhood.
The public park — planted squarely in the middle
of the neighborhood and bounded by the public high
school on one side, the Catholic church on another,
and a small tightly-knit Italian-American community
on the other two sides — was destined to become the
center of tensions among the youth of our neighborhood.

Before we look at the impact of racial tension on
teenagers, however, let us go back a few years in history to see briefly the traditions and youth patterns
that marked our neighborhood during its more stable
years. It is only in that kind of context that we will
be able to observe the subtle but significant changes
that came over our young people during the days of
racial transition.

Grand Crossing Park on the Southeast Side of
Chicago has had a noble past. Although it was not
my privilege to grow up in this area, I have heard
many stories of the athletic prowess of the boys from
Grand Crossing. I doubt if there is another neighborhood in the city of Chicago that has had such an en-
viable record of competitive sports. Outstanding
athletic teams, fierce competitors, championship-type
athletes — this has been the tradition of Grand Crossing, reaching as far back as any an old-timer would

care to remember. Some of the great contests and great athletes continue to live on in the memory of the people.

The significant thing about the athletic tradition of Grand Crossing is that the park — geographically — was in the very heart of an Italian-American settlement, and most of the outstanding young athletes were of Italian origin. The athletes of today were carrying on the glories their fathers and uncles had won in years past. In such a tradition, it was quite natural that these young champions should consider Grand Crossing Park as their own park, a place they were terribly jealous and proud of. The stories still linger on of how fifteen and twenty years ago the boys from Grand Crossing protected the park from the invasion of the Irish or Germans — or anyone with "blond" hair.

The strong athletic tradition of the young people of Grand Crossing was a good thing. The boys had a lot of pride; they stuck rather closely together; they seldom if ever bothered anybody; they never roamed around other neighborhoods looking for trouble; they had no problems of delinquency. They were a proud, haughty, high-minded type of young people. In everything they set their athletic prowess to, they came in first.

I detail this tradition of Grand Crossing at this time, because this is the backdrop to the entrance of the Negro into our community.

When the Negro first began moving into the community in the vicinity of the park, it was obvious that racial crises would sooner or later be provoked among the young people of Grand Crossing. Not knowing the background and patterns of the new community in which they were moving, the Negro youth very normally — and rightfully — set their eyes on the park. They wanted to use it.

Simultaneously, the public high school adjacent to the park began to reflect the racial change in the neighborhood. The youth problem was now being posed on two fronts — the park and the public high school.

Let us look more deeply into what was beginning to take place in the minds and hearts — the attitudes — of the young people.

First of all, with the entrance of the Negro into this previously very stable and well-established community, the adults were the first to push the panic button. For the first time in several generations, the community was threatened from without. All of the fears about declining real estate values, crime and vice, slums, and so forth found expression among the adults. The conversation — whether at dinner table in the family circle, on the street, in the shopping centers, over the back fences, in taverns, at church gatherings in schools — became charged with mounting racial tension. Insecurity, fears, suspicions, hatreds, rumors filled the air.

Quite naturally, all of this would be caught up by the young people in the neighborhood. For the first time in many years, the young people could identify a common enemy. They felt themselves called to some kind of Holy War — to defend their community, their property, their traditions, their families, and their women. Here was a cause that stirred their competitive instincts as no athletic contest had ever done before. The matter was posed in terms of a life and death struggle of a community, and the park would become the battleground. The youth became restless. The adults stood behind their offspring in any action they might take to keep the enemy from taking over. The battles that were fought verbally by adults in conversation were also to be fought bodily by their children in the park, on street corners, or wherever a threat arose.

A noticeable change in attitude came over the young people. A subtle but telling disrespect for law and order was setting in. Restlessness, cockiness, gang spirit, tension characterized them. An increase in petty delinquencies took place — fights, robberies, car strippings, drinking parties, and other acts that were literally unknown in the community in the past now became frequent. New gangs and groups — over and above the traditional athletic clubs were forming; the young people seemed to be out on the prowl more in cars, on street corners, in club houses. A serious youth problem was mounting in the community. Not all of it was racial, by any means.

During all this time, Negroes were moving in block after block. While the change was slow in the area immediately surrounding the park (some blocks have yet to change) because of the single-family character of the area, not so in the densely populated apartment area south of the park, where change took place almost overnight. The result of all the change was that the number of White youth continually declined in the neighborhood, while the number of Negro youth steadily increased, to a point where the Negro youth now are in the majority.

It is not my intention to chronicle all the little racial fires that broke out over a several-year span in the community: nothing of really serious enough nature to provoke an all-out race riot, but a continuous string of incidents — garage burnings, fights, gang fights prearranged by both sides, bullet-slinging, etc. The only saving feature of the situation was the fact that as time wore on, the White kids matured, got tired of an endless string of incidents, became outnumbered, and eventually began to concede ground on the matter. In the end, most of the trouble was caused by White youth returning to the neighborhood — after having moved out — still fired up with some kind of mission to save it for those who still lived there.

Little by little, almost inch by inch, the Negroes have moved into the park. First, the tennis courts and play lots, then the softball and baseball diamonds, the swimming pool, and now the basketball courts in the fieldhouse. Little by little, almost inch by inch, the White boys have pulled back, given in, and faced the stark realities of the situation. The past is gone; the traditions are gone; the park is gone; the community is gone. A new age has dawned. What it will be like they are not sure, but they seem resigned — those who still remain. Maybe it is because they too — psychologically — have their bags already packed.

Setting aside the racial nature of the problem momentarily, I would like to make a few observations on what has happened to the young people in our community in the past several years. As one who was very active among and closely identified with the youth of our community even before the racial problem posed itself, I have seen the change in the community and in the attitudes of our youth. I have seen the rise of youth delinquencies and the breakdown of morale among the young.

Through all this I could not help but feel very sad about it and not help but become demoralized myself. I believe strongly in stability — in strong traditions of home, Church, neighborhood, family — and I have seen disintegration take place in all these institutions which normally should be havens of security and stability in the difficult times of adolecscence. This has inflicted a terrible blow on the moral fibre of our young people. It is not for me to blame these young teenagers, emotionally unequipped to deal with the almost traumatic upheaval that came into their lives at a time when they had not yet developed the maturity to cope with it or even understand what was taking place.

I know I will never forget the night at our parish youth social when I came across a strapping young boy sitting all alone in the corner of the hall, almost with tears in his eyes. As I sat down next to him and began to probe for the problem, he looked up and said simply: "This is the saddest day of my life." And I knew at a glance why the day was so sad. It was the day his family had moved out of our neighborhood into another one some distance away — because Negroes had moved into their block.

This incident is one I was to experience over and over again among the teenagers in our community as they moved out. To be suddenly uprooted from the community, the associations, the activities, the friendships they had known all their life and to be transplanted into a completely different community is not an easy experience for most people. While I am convinced of the marvelous adaptability of youth and know that in time they will quickly readjust to new circumstances, I feel that this experience has a profound effect on many of these youth at a time when they are not quite able to cope with it emotionally.

I know that my own home has become a kind of home away from home for countless young people moved out, as they return week after week to their old neighborhood and use my home as a kind of place to hang their hats while they are back. I have been especially lenient in letting them look upon my house as such a haven because of the tremendous sensitivity

I have to the problem they are experiencing. In time they readjust and their trips back become less frequent, but during that difficult interim period I am consoled if I can be of some help.

To see these young people, who were once so carefree and full of the innocence we have learned to admire in youth, gradually become corrupted spiritually by fears and hatreds; to see their idealism replaced by a kind of cynicism towards human beings; to see a kind of enjoyment in them over inflicting harm on people and property; to see developing in them a kind of racial superiority that closes off almost all inspirations of Christian charity, respect, mercy, justice, meekness, and humility — these are experiences that I will never forget. I cannot help but wonder what kind of adults these youths will eventually become. What kind of citizens? What kind of Christians? What kind of parents? How deeply have these cancers of hatred and fear cut into their spirit? How quickly they have grown up and hardened!

How can I ever forget the evening I was walking over to the parish to conduct a Confraternity of Christian Doctrine course for public high school students. Suddenly, I was confronted with a gang of boys, fifteen and sixteen years of age, armed with bottles, bats, chains, sticks with nails protruding through — all very carefully made for the occasion. When I noticed that most of the boys were students of our Confraternity program, I asked them what they were up to. In a blasé way, they told me they would be a little late for

51

their instruction this evening, for they had a little project to take care of. They were out "to clean up the neighborhood," as one boy phrased it in almost missionary terms. They were to meet a group of Negro boys at a certain vacant lot for a skirmish. The cold, matter-of-fact way they informed me; the quiet self-confidence they had in themselves and in their mission; the glaring incongruity between engaging in such an antisocial act and their religious instruction — these things astounded me.

Weak-kneed, I continued on to the church to ask one of the priests to get in his car and follow them. As it turned out, the Negro gang never kept its appointment with destiny, and true to their word, the boys were all back in the classroom for their instruction — ten minutes late.

When I look back on the almost nightmarish few years of youth work in a changing neighborhood, I begin to see how easy it was for a Hitler or a Mussolini to fire up a nation with a spirit of racial superiority. I wonder if someday a demagogue — unless we find a way to solve our racial problems — might not be able to do the same thing in America? The youth I have been associated with are not delinquent; they are from good solid families; they are about as typical a group of teenagers that one would find anywhere in America's urban centers. They are products of our school system — Catholic and public. They are middle-class — not the products of slums, overcrowded housing, and bad environmental conditions.

To the credit of our democratic institutions, several constructive programs have developed in our neighborhood the past several years which have played no small part in easing our youth through the crisis of racial change without any serious race riot or outbreak or even loss of life.

Over and above the workings of the Holy Spirit and the overtime work of guardian angels, the community has responded in several ways to admit some rays of hope into the situation and offer a good omen for the future in other neighborhoods when and as they confront the same kind of problem.

Through the past five years, our parish has had some strong youth activities and programs that played no small role in helping our youth in a time of crisis. A Confraternity of Christian Doctrine program for public high school students, groups of Young Christian Students and Young Christian Workers, and a parish teenage social club — all of them involving apostolic-minded priests and laity — have been in operation, often in a quiet but still effective way. Through these activities, we never hoped to achieve much more than to neutralize the young people on the race question — to prevent open warfare and to get them to think at least twice before engaging in some antisocial act. Countless small group meetings, which consisted in Gospel discussions and inquiries into the problems of youth in our parish — and a few constructive actions have been successful in bringing many of these problems out on the table under the light of Christian teaching. Heated but at least free, uninhibited discussion of the racial problem time and time again has in varying degrees had a significant effect on the attitude of many young adults and teenagers in our parish. Some few have gone on to almost heroic acts of leadership in these movements. From the long-range point of view — and of tremendous help to our parish at the moment — a significant number of young people, some now married, some still single, have made a kind of long-range commitment to our parish and the neighborhood, to work with the priests in their overpowering task of seeing the parish through this painful period of transition. The reserve of apostolic leaders now in our parish — willing and anxious to lend their hand to CCD programs, youth programs, community associations, convert-making projects, parish societies — is gradually helping our parish come back to life. Those are people who have made some kind of commitment towards working for an integrated community. How successful their efforts will be remains yet to be seen.

At least the youth know the parish has not abandoned them, has not lost interest in them. The young people know there is a small but dedicated group of young adults in the parish who are their friends, who can be trusted, who can be called upon in time of need, who will treat them with sympathy and understanding and kindness. They know the priests of the parish are behind them and interested in them, and that the parish is at their service. These may be small gains but they are a moderating influence on the emotions of these young people.

The other assist has come, quite unexpectedly but nevertheless gratifyingly, from a new and exciting program developed by the YMCA in Chicago as an effort to reach the youth in our inner city faced with serious problems of a delinquent or gang nature. Very simply the YMCA has developed a program — out of its downtown office — whereby detached youth workers or neighborhood workers are assigned full-time to neighborhoods where study shows an existing teenage problem or a potentiality for some kind of delinquency.

Supported by trained youth workers and backed by a continuing sociological research project at the University of Chicago, the YMCA program is a pilot project only a few years old. Already it has some ten field workers — some Negro and some White — assigned to various Chicago neighborhoods where in the opinion of the project some help is needed.

Two years ago a White youth worker was assigned by the YMCA to the Grand Crossing area in view of the developing racial tensions there and increase of petty crimes. The particular worker assigned to our area, a graduate of Notre Dame in sociology, tied in at once with existing programs in the community — the various youth activities of our parish being especially helpful to his work. He quickly found a group of young Catholic youth workers and leaders — products of the Young Christian Workers and

Young Christian Students in our parish — to work with in a team effort at solving some of the basic problems all of us saw developing in Grand Crossing.

As a neighborhood worker, our youth specialist spent his time in the neighborhood working closely with the young people, identifying with them, winning their confidence, being of assistance to them, and in general helping them develop projects and programs which would direct their activities and energies along constructive lines. He was not associated with any particular YMCA center, but on his own worked with and through whatever community facilities and organizations exist for the youth of the area.

Various kinds of athletic leagues and contests — both within our community and also among teams from other neighborhoods in Chicago where the YMCA has youth workers assigned — have been one direct result of his activities. Bowling, softball, swimming, pool-shooting, basketball programs have been successfully organized, with the result that many young people, normally not athletically inclined, have become interested in sports and have found new outlets for their energies. Some boys with antisocial tendencies have taken on new personalities, once accepted and integrated into athletic programs.

One year a bowling league was organized which brought together four teams representing four different groups of boys in the neighborhood, with the result that tensions that previously existed between these groups were dissolved. Topped off with a bowling banquet, presentation of trophies, and a dance, the bowling program generated a good spirit among the youth of the neighborhood.

One summer in a significant pilot project, a softball league was organized among some ten neighborhoods in Chicago where YMCA workers were active. An Inner City Softball Tournament — twenty-six games for each team, playing twice a week — brought together for the first time, for example, two White teams from Grand Crossing and Negro teams from other parts of the city. As a first step towards integration, the competition found Negro and White teams playing together in friendly rivalry and without incident. In fact many side games were scheduled between Negro teams and the teams from Grand Crossing over and above the regular league games. The one team from Grand Crossing, keeping intact its long tradition, won the league and the playoffs, while the other team from Grand Crossing won the sportsmanship trophies.

As part of the over-all YMCA project, an employment service was set up by a competent director, with the result that many of the boys in our neighborhood who had not completed high school and thus found it difficult to locate jobs, are now working regularly. Another program whereby these boys will be able to finish their high school education is now being investigated. These are all concrete services which have benefited the youth of our neighborhood.

On a person-to-person basis the YMCA worker in our neighborhood has been able to help many boys straighten out — those who got into trouble as well as those treading on the borderline of trouble. He has been able to be on top of all situations, calm tensions, redirect activities, be a friend in court, intercede with parents, and so on. He has been able to do all those things that need being done in almost every neighborhood but which are not done simply because no one can give all his time to them. In a way, it has been as though our parish has had a full-time youth worker in the past two years.

We shudder to think what explosive situations would have developed in our changing neighborhood the past several years had not a dedicated youth worker been constantly on the scene working hand in glove with what activities we were able to develop through the parish. That we have come through this difficult transition period as well as we have is due in no small part to the efforts of this youth worker.

IV

REORGANIZING THE COMMUNITY

Two Protestant ministers, a Catholic priest, an optometrist, a civil servant, a businessman, a housewife, and a publisher were gathered together at the home of the president of the West Avalon Community Association. Representing both Negroes and Whites, this small group composed the board of directors of the association. Once a month the group met in the home of one of the members to plan the affairs of the association.

Over a period of months, the group had jelled together as an effective instrument for community action. Initial strangeness or uneasiness among members of a group drawn together by circumstances and common interests in the community of Grand Crossing and Chatham has gradually dissolved. A good deal of free and easy repartee bandies back and forth among the members. The ministers are relaxed and able to chide each other; the Negroes and Whites have developed a permissive relationship in which almost anything can be said without fear of offense. To put it briefly, the board of the West Avalon Community Association reflects a healthy relationship between a group of community leaders regardless of race, creed, or national origin. We hope it will someday be symbolic of the relationships that exist in the community among the people.

On the agenda of this particular monthly meeting were some routine as well as some significant items, some of which were controversial even among the board members. Some were matters of practical decision — timing, the when and how to achieve certain goals. As I recall the meeting — which was not an unusual but a typical one — a large part of it was concerned with planning a monthly membership meeting on the subject of open occupancy legislation for the state of Illinois. Legislation providing for freedom of residence among all citizens regardless of race, creed or national origin had been proposed both in the state legislature at Springfield and in the City Council of Chicago. The legislation had been the subject of much discussion.

The West Avalon Community Association had decided to conduct an educational meeting for its members on the pending legislation, not so much to take a stand as an association for or against the legislation as to hold a public airing of it and hear all the pros and cons for it. We felt our people were not informed on the details of the legislation being proposed. We could perform a service by conducting an open meeting on the matter to which the general public would be invited. As we discussed the program at our board meeting, the panel-discussion idea began to jell. We would invite Negro and White participants on both the pro and con side of the legislation. By presenting both sides, we felt we could best appeal to all the residents of our community and show our own interest in the welfare of all.

The proposed meeting on open occupancy was typical of the kind of programming we had tried to have at our monthly meetings. In the past year and a half, we had provided some interesting programs centered on problems pertaining to our own geographic area. In most instances, we attempted to draw upon our own community resources for speakers and panelists rather than appeal to downtown agencies for programs. The West Avalon Community Association, in our minds, would be most effective if it bore down on local problems and did not deal in broad generalities.

Furthermore, we were not organized specifically as a brotherhood group — to promote better relations between different racial and religious groups — although this would certainly be a by-product of our work. Our primary purpose was to deal with local community problems, to mobilize the residents within our boundaries to confront the problems posed in a changing neighborhood. We felt we could best bring people together in action programs and around specific issues rather than around ideological issues.

It was our feeling that too many community organizations, operating out of a kind of inferiority complex on the race-relations issue, spent more of their time promoting better race relations and brotherhood, in a kind of sentimental way, than in solving ticklish community problems, such as illegal conversions, overcrowding, violations of city ordinances regarding health, safety, fire and building codes, violations of zoning ordinances, and a host of other problems attendant upon rapid racial change in a community. To the extent we could unite the residents to solve these problems would our organization be effective.

Among some of the monthly educational programs we sponsored were talks by: the alderman; the local police district captain on police protection in the area and crime rates; the ward superintendent on questions such as garbage disposal, street cleaning, and street lighting; block club organizers from other community associations, to share their success and failure and techniques and experience at organizing block clubs; representatives of all agencies in the community working with youth — school officials, youth workers, ministers, and teenage leaders themselves; representatives of the Chicago zoning department to discuss the question of rezoning parts of our community. These are some of the programs the West Avalon Community Association sponsored for the residents of the area the past year.

Not only does the monthly membership meeting of the association serve as an educational forum for the residents, but it also enables them to report in on community problems they would like to see solved. Everything from abandoned cars on the streets to an influx of taverns, liquor stores, gaming houses, or houses of prostitution are brought to the attention of the association for action. Through regularized complaint forms, citizens can file specific complaints, which the association in turn will refer to the proper city agency for disposal. In this way, the individual making the complaint can remain anonymous, whereas the association, with its collective strength, can pursue the case and generally get prompt action. Whereas a single citizen complaining to City Hall may not get much of a hearing (he is only one vote) an association represents a power block in the community. Politicians, it seems, are very sensitive to power blocks.

Last year when the West Avalon Community Association attempted to work for a rezoning of a certain ten-block area within its boundaries from one classification, which would allow large apartment buildings to be built in the area, to a lower classification, which would preserve the single family character of the area, the residents had to be mobilized. First of all, a land survey committee was formed to study the present housing characteristics of the area in order to present a detailed map of existing structures to the zoning department of the city.

Once the land survey was completed, a presentation was made to the zoning department for an opinion from them on the merits of our case for an amendment of current zoning regulations. With the support of the local alderman, we were given a hearing before a special committee of the City Council. We presented our case, showed our survey, presented petitions which we had secured from the residents in the area, and asked our alderman to defend our case. As a result, we won the case and the ordinance was so amended, only the second such amendment in Chicago.

What the amendment means, very simply, is that no new large apartment buildings can be erected in our area unless some very stringent conditions are met as to frontage, space per person, parking facilities, etc. It also prevents boarding houses, hotels, and rest homes from opening up in the area. The single-family character of the area will be preserved and the density of population will be controlled. With the prevention of overcrowding, which would accompany apartment construction, many community problems will be averted.

This is a very concrete example of what a community association can achieve once the residents get behind it and support it. The people living in this small, ten-block area could not have accomplished their goal working alone. They needed the support and strength of the larger community association. The West Avalon Community Association represented enough strength to guarantee the support of our alderman. His support in turn carried weight with the City Council committee which decided our case.

To return to our typical board meeting of the West Avalon Community Association, a second topic on our agenda this particular evening was "Block Clubs." To our edification but surprise, some eight or ten block clubs had spontaneously come into existence during the past year. I say that we were surprised because we actually had not made any provisions in the by-laws of our association for block clubs when we first organized. Our membership was set up on an individual basis only, so long as the members lived in the area we serve and so long as they paid two dollars a year membership dues.

It has not been the experience in community organizations in all-White communities that the people formed block clubs. Since the West Avalon association was organized originally by a dominantly White leadership, the question of block clubs never entered our minds. What a pleasant surprise, then, to find the Negro leaders in our fast-changing community so enthusiastic about block clubs. Many of them brought the experience of block clubs from the previous neighborhood they had lived in. It was only natural for them to want to form them again in their new community.

Just what is a block club and why is it so important to a community? Contrary to what some people may think, a block club is not a social or fraternal organization, although sociability may be one of its by-products. Actually, people have enough social life among friends and relatives without needing to go out into the block to form social clubs. Instead, block clubs are organized primarily to watchdog eyesores or ordinance violations on a certain street. They are composed of community-minded residents of a block who believe that by banding together they can preserve high community standards in the block and also educate their neighbors to an interest in the community into which they have just moved.

A block club is formed by one or two spirited residents in the community who simply canvass their block to introduce the idea to their neighbors. They call a meeting in someone's home or basement, elect officers, set dues and by-laws, and begin work on some existing problem in the block. It may mean that the men will get together on a Saturday morning to clean up a vacant lot which has gathered litter, or conduct a paint-up campaign for garbage disposal units along the alley, or even purchase garbage disposal cans for those who don't have them. It may mean a joint effort to raise some funds for a snow plow which all the members will be entitled to use, or to convert a vacant lot into a playlot for the children. And of course, if anyone drives through the South Side of Chicago during the Christmas holidays and discovers certain streets gaily lighted and decorated, he can be sure a block club is active on that street.

Block clubs can do a fine job of educating people in basic principles of urban living. When one family was regularly burning garbage, a block club committee called upon them for a friendly visit and simply explained this was illegal and was causing an odor on the street. The offenders were grateful for the information and discontinued the practice immediately. This particular family simply was not accustomed to urban living.

When one man's home was robbed one day, I recall

one of our block club leaders asking the victim if he belonged to a block club. He replied that there was no block club on his street. The other fellow suggested that had there been an active block organization, chances are the burglars would have been noticed and apprehended. His point was well-taken. Block clubs are good watchdogs because their members have learned to observe their block and know their neighbors. They know when strangers enter the neighborhood. They are alert to anything strange or unusual in the block. As a result, they help police the area. Everyone in the block benefits from this.

Block clubs have one inherent problem, however, which only a broader-based community association can solve. They need to be a part of something larger than themselves, to be affiliated with a larger community association, or they will inevitably die on the vine. Unless the members of a block club are associated in broader community problems, they will become parochial and turn inward. The club will as a consequence be difficult to sustain. After all, there are only so many housekeeping problems that can be solved on a particular block. After the initial burst of enthusiasm, what is there to sustain the club and keep up its community interest? This is the basic question.

When block clubs are a part of a larger community association, however, their members can participate in community-wide projects, many of which affect the local block: for example, police protection or garbage collection or street lighting. A single block club by itself is somewhat helpless in facing this kind of problem, but not so if it is a member of a larger organization. Block clubs also have built-in abilities to raise funds; in fact fund-raising in itself can help hold the club together. They can be very useful, then, in helping to raise funds for the larger association so that it can carry on its broader community action and education.

On the other side of the coin, larger community associations desperately need block clubs. They need a grass-roots membership. They need the excellent channels of communication from the top down to the local citizen which block clubs can provide. Block clubs can become the sounding board for ideas and projects for the larger association, so that it keeps in touch with the needs of the community and always be atuned to the feelings and thoughts of the residents. Out of block clubs will emerge leadership talent for the larger association. Block clubs can be a kind of training ground for people who are willing to assume larger community responsibilities.

An ideal community association, therefore, ought to provide for individual membership for all block club members as well as for institutional membership, with voting privileges, for the block clubs themselves. A special committee within the larger organization of block club representatives ought to be activated. This was the way, in fact, that we discussed the question of block clubs at our typical board meeting in an effort to find a happy solution to the problem of incorporating block clubs into our West Avalon Community Association. We need block clubs, and they need us.

It was quite natural that we also discussed the matter of funds at this particular meeting, for fund-raising and block clubs are very closely related. Furthermore, there was the matter of getting businesses and other institutions in the community incorporated into the West Avalon Community Association. An effective community association needs the support of all the institutions in the area — businesses, Churches, schools, fraternal and civic organizations, and block clubs — if it is to be representative of the community and if it is to raise the necessary funds for carrying on its work.

Businesses in particular are essential to a good community association. Out of their own enlightened self-interest, local merchants ought to support a community association. After all, if they are to stay in this community and develop their business and make a profit, they must be intensely interested in what kind of community it is going to be, in whether or not community standards will attract a high type of resident and other legitimate businesses, or whether the community will deteriorate to a kind which attracts all kinds of riff-raffs, loan sharks, liquor distributors, store front Churches — in effect all the slum symbols whose interest is in making quick and dishonest dollars off the residents.

A community association is able to develop a sense of confidence in the community, so that legitimate businessmen will want to open up in the area. It is also able to develop a sense of confidence in the people toward the local merchants. If the residents expect legitimate business to come into the area and stay there, they must be educated to support local businessmen and not, for example, continue to return to their old neighborhoods to do business. Much education must be done along these lines to show the people the long-range advantages to them and to the community if they patronize their local merchants.

The president of the West Avalon Community Association is a local merchant. He is also a dedicated community leader. He is active in civic affairs, the PTA, fraternal organizations, his Church, the YMCA, and he also lives in the community. He is the kind of high-minded leader and resident and businessman our community desperately needs. But if he cannot make a success of his business in this area — that is, if the local people do not patronize him — we run the risk of losing him as a resident as well as a local merchant. The loss of such a man to the community would be tragic. It is not simply a question of bringing businesses into the association in order to get contributions from them for financing the work of the association. It is a question of enlisting their leadership, their judgment, their interest, and their sense of community responsibility. These are assets on which no price tags can be placed.

The problem of financing a voluntary community association, such as ours, is not an easy one. It seems to revolve around the kind of association the residents want. The more the association probes into the many problems involved in creating a new community, the more helpless it tends to feel without the help of paid and trained personnel — at least the help of a full-time executive secretary who can attend to the endless details and complications involved in community work.

The West Avalon Community Association is a voluntary grouping together of residents interested in maintaining a good, stable community. Its officers and board members are ordinary neighbors who have their own livelihoods to earn, families to raise, and activities to pursue. To demand or even expect of them the kind of long and involved man-hours of meetings, and activities in between meetings, and follow-ups on violations and planning is utopian. Can they attend to all the problems competently on a kind of hit and run basis, or must they work towards some kind of staff personnel? So much of the work involved is bird-dogging out problems which city and county agencies are negligent in solving, and so much of the work, also, involves the long and tedious democratic processes out of which some kind of consensus of opinion must always emerge before action can be taken or policies fixed.

On the other hand, a staff — and all that implies in terms of salary and overhead — is financially prohibitive if membership dues are the main source of revenue. Either high-powered fund-raising campaigns

71

must be launched, with an assist from foundations and welfare associations, or the work simply cannot be done. This problem is by no means unique to the West Avalon Community Association. Every community organization in Chicago faces it.

One pattern being followed today — and it may yet be too early to gauge its success — is for community associations in a given area to band together into a supra-community organization. The supra-organization will raise funds on a large scale and set up an office and a staff, whose task it will be to serve the various member associations. The member associations, meanwhile, will preserve their own autonomy but continue to function as unstaffed associations.

This pattern was very much on the minds of the board members of the West Avalon at our typical board meeting. Within recent months two supra-organizations of community action have been organized on the South Side of Chicago. To the West of our boundaries, an organization for the entire southwest side of Chicago has been developed the past two years. To the east of our boundaries, a similar effort to organize the entire southeast side of Chicago into a supra-organization is now being made. Our own West Avalon Community Association recently became affiliated with SECO, the South East Community Organization.

There is a deeper reason than financial behind this recent trend towards supra-organizations on Chicago's South Side. First of all, no one is happy with the steady development of one all-Negro neighborhood after another on the South Side, as neighborhood after neighborhood panics in the face of racial change and eventually becomes dominantly Negro, if not all Negro. How long will this continue to happen? How long will it be before the South Side of Chicago becomes dominantly Negro? How long will it be before Chicago will be a dominantly Negro city rimmed with White suburbs? Somehow and somewhere an effort must be made to stop this trend and create a climate in which Whites will not panic and flee and in which some kind of integrated community can be successfully developed.

The formation of the broad-based organization for the Southwest Community is an effort to stem this tide. It is founded on the idea that if people are properly prepared for the inevitable racial change and if the community takes certain steps to prepare itself for the peaceful advent of the Negro, perhaps the residents will face up to their unrealistic but traditional position of trying to "keep 'em out" which has failed time and time again, and instead accept the fact that integration is here to stay — if anyone expects to live out his life in the big city.

Closely tied to the need for this kind of re-evaluation, is the need for a broad community-education program to condition the people for the eventual changes which are to come so that change will be orderly and not disruptive of an entire community, as has been the case in the past. Also, the community must remain attractive to the present residents and financially attractive to young families in particular, who often are compelled to flee to the suburbs simply because they cannot afford to buy housing within the city limits. Older houses must be modernized and placed on the market at prices which young families can afford and also finance with small down-payments. Real estate operators, banks and mortgage houses, community and civic organizations, Churches and schools — all the institutions within the area must be mobilized into this gigantic effort to save the city of Chicago, and to save most of our large urban centers.

In the past, small neighborhood community groups have often been organized on the unwritten but effective "keep the Negroes out" basis. The so-called improvement organizations, ostensibly organized to stabilize the community and maintain community standards, too often have been veiled attempts to draw hard and fast boundaries beyond which Negroes were never to pass. Organized primarily among home-owners and businesses, the strategy for these organizations has been to convince the residents not to sell to Negroes, and in fact, to try to pool resources in order to buy "threatened" property in the name of the association or to make a concerted effort to see that vacancies, when they arise, are filled with Whites. This has been the general philosophy behind improvement organizations.

Inevitably, these organizations fail in their objectives. Inevitably, some so-called "greedy" resident becomes the first to sell to Negroes. Since the improvement association has done nothing to condition the people to this eventuality, but instead promised that it would never happen, panic follows. When one sells, the dike is opened. Within a relatively short time, the neighborhood undergoes radical change. And once again, boundary lines are redrawn, a new improvement association forms, and the whole process is begun anew. And again there is nothing but failure, and in fact the very reverse of what was hoped for happens. These are the bare facts of the situation and have nothing to do with whether or not one is a segregationist or an integrationist, as the charges are so often made.

The problem of the stabilization of a community has always fascinated me. On both sides — the "keep them out" *improvement* organizations and the "bring them in" *community* associations — have argued for stability. There has been unanimity among them on community standards, keeping the community a nice place to live in, adequately policed and serviced by city agencies, developing community pride and spirit. There is no question that both sides are in agreement on these very worthwhile goals.

The difference seems to lie in this. The *improvement* organization would achieve stability by preserving the present homogeneous character of a community, on the basis that once Negroes or Puerto Ricans or any other outside group is allowed in, the community will automatically decline, deteriorate, and degenerate into a slum area. Property values will go down, people will lose on their investment, and in the turnover the present community as they know it will disintegrate. Because improvement organizations are composed mostly of property-owners and businessmen, they are obviously motivated by vested interests — which explains so much of their zeal and closed thinking on the matter. Mortgage houses, savings and loan associations, real estate operators of the legitimate kind, all back up this view that homogeneity is the answer. Politicians certainly are not anxious to see anything happen which will affect the present constituency of their ward or district. With this kind of support, improvement organizations are formidable.

On the other hand, the *community* association in the past has usually come into existence upon the heels of improvement organizations. Its basic conviction is that improvement organizations are doomed to failure, no matter how much support they muster, that in fact Chicago history shows that not once has an improvement organization achieved its goal on the South Side. Neighborhood after neighborhood in which they have operated have "lost the battle," as it were, and racial turnover has come about. Boundary lines have been drawn and redrawn, without success. How long shall this continue?

With failure to maintain segregation an obvious fact, the community association argues the other side of the coin. Let there be integration. "We want neither all-White or all-Negro neighborhoods. Both are bad for Chicago's future and both are indefensible in a democracy. Let us therefore try to stabilize a community on an interracial basis. Let us allay fears." The argument is advanced that if the people know in advance that integration is coming, that it is part of urban life today, perhaps they can learn to live with the eventuality and begin to realize that it may not be as horrible as it was painted by the improvement advocates but in fact may be very enriching.

Community associations argue that in fact stability — the goals on which all such efforts agree — can be achieved only if the community association is representative of all the people of the community, regardless of race, creed, color or national origin. Community associations point with pride to the fact that, contrary to fears and rumors, the incoming Negro residents by and large have a high degree of community spirit — perhaps higher than that of the Whites whom they displace, as witnessed by their interest in block clubs, for example. In point of fact, the newcomers will guarantee the eventual success of the community association. They are ripe for new responsibilities as home-owners or as members of a community that is no longer a ghetto but has a chance of being open and free, to which they as Americans are entitled. They seize upon these very strong personal motivating factors to work energetically and selflessly at this business of community-building.

This is where the battle for stability is being fought today. It all depends upon one's point of view. It will be fought out along these lines in the supra-organizations as well as on the local neighborhood level or even in the block club. In fact, I suspect that people within a single family argue the matter out pretty much in the same terms. The consoling feature about it all is that we are all united on the principle of stability. How to achieve it is the only point of difference. Until we get this difference out into the open, it will not be resolved.

It is to be hoped that the supra-organizations, with enlightened leadership, can build confidence in the people, reduce their fears and doubts through education, keep their doors open to all newcomers, regardless of race, religion, or national origin, and set up some community standards which all newcomers will have to meet in order to become a part of the community. This should be the broad philosophy behind the supra-organizations. Actually, these organizations are in a death struggle on the South Side of Chicago for the future of the city, whether the residents realize this or not. ▷If the effort fails, we will have lost the urban battle and we will have lost face around the world in our manner of handling race relations. The whole world is watching.◁

To say this much is not to place a halo around the leaders of these supra-organizations; it is not to hail them as the messiahs. To date the two efforts cited above have had hard and vigorous intramural battles over the best approaches to the problem. Without a doubt some of the members — and leaders — of the supra-organizations think it is still essentially another "keep them out" attempt except on a broader scale. The prevailing philosophy will have to win out in the conference room, at committee and officers' meetings and in the public forum. It will require high-level politicking to gain the day for democracy. The democratic process itself will be on trial, but through it all we can only be optimistic, for democracy will be at work.

I detail these things only to illustrate the kind of community battles now being fought out on the South Side of Chicago. These battles are of tremendous importance to the whole of Chicago, to our nation, and to the image of America abroad. How well a large urban center such as Chicago can come to grips with the racial problem at the community level is in many ways the measure of America's moral strength as well as the strength of the democratic principle. These are grass-roots problems being fought out in the neighborhoods of Chicago. Through the institutions that emerge from all this will be refracted the image of America — let there be no doubt about this.

The West Avalon Community Association is a small part of the total fabric. It is a struggling effort born in pain out of a failing improvement organization that tried for ten years to stabilize an area but failed. Today the West Avalon Association is integrated. Perhaps tomorrow it will be dominantly Negro because its effort was made too late. Perhaps it will fail completely. Nonetheless it already has achieved some good in the community; it has given a kind of testimony to the effort that ought to be made in many other parts of Chicago — and other large cities — only the next time before it is already too late. Its experience is an open book for others to read — and perhaps take a lesson or two away from. There are no easy or quick solutions to these tremendous human problems. Perhaps an ideal integrated community is ten or twenty years away. But in the life of a city, ten or twenty years is really not a very long time at all.

The quiet meeting of a small integrated group composed of two Protestant ministers, a Catholic priest, an optometrist, a civil servant, a businessman, a housewife, and a publisher sitting as members of the board of the West Avalon Community Association one evening last year may not have been historic. But we think it was a step in the right direction.

V

MISSION OF THE CHURCH

Although no one would ever use the boxes of Sunday envelopes given out to Catholic parishioners each year as an index to the spiritual life of the Catholic Church in the United States, the distribution of these envelopes can tell us a few things about the rise or decline of Church membership. The Sunday offering is one index most parishes can rely upon in estimating the number of practical Catholics within its boundaries.

At St. Francis de Paula Catholic church in the Grand Crossing-Chatham area of Chicago, 4,500 boxes of Sunday envelopes were distributed in 1958, one of the peak years in the history of this Catholic parish. Those 4,500 boxes of Sunday envelopes probably represented some eight or nine thousand adult Catholics in our community at that time, with some allowances made for noncontributors, lax or fallen-away Catholics. This would come close to about 50 per cent of the population within the parish boundaries.

During that same year of 1958, the grammar school operated by the parish had its largest enrollment — some 650 students — cared for by eleven Sisters and three lay teachers. In addition to the monsignor-pastor, there were three priests as full-time assistants and two priests part-time in the parish. St. Francis de Paula in 1958 could be called a typical large urban parish in a predominantly middle-class neighborhood, with a church, rectory, school and convent fully modernized and paid for.

In December of 1960, exactly three years later, 1,500 boxes of Sunday envelopes were distributed, or three thousand boxes less than in 1958, representing an estimated loss of some six thousand adult Catholics in three years. In simple statistics and using the most accurate gauge available — the much maligned Sunday envelope — this is the story of racial change in Grand Crossing-Chatham as it effects the Catholic Church.

Since 1959 St. Francis de Paula has been under the pastoral guidance of a new pastor, the old monsignor having died, perhaps from a broken heart at seeing his parish dwindle away. Today there are two full-time assistants in the parish in addition to the pastor, along with two priests in residence who have part-time duties in the parish. The school is still in operation but at about two-thirds capacity and staffed by the Franciscan Sisters, with the help of several lay teachers. The school is approximately 85 per cent Negro in its present enrollment.

As the White parishioners move out of the parish in face of quick racial change, they are displaced by Negroes who are only about 6 per cent Catholic as compared to the 50 per cent Catholic population among the Whites. Today St. Francis de Paula shows in its Church membership a roughly estimated 20 per cent Negro—80 per cent White membership. Despite the fact that the neighborhood is largely Negro, the Catholic Church remains dominantly White. While the White people are a minority in the community, the Negroes are a minority in the Church. The Negroes at this point still view St. Francis de Paula as a White man's church; they have yet to achieve a real sense of identity with the parish and probably will not do so until they become the majority in the parish and in parish organizations.

The Catholic Church finds herself in a somewhat different position in the community than any of the Protestant congregations. As is immediately obvious, the Catholic Church has enjoyed the key position, numerically speaking, among the various Churches, both before and after the racial transition. While the Catholic Church is geographical — which means all of her parishioners live immediately within the boundaries of the community — Protestant Churches are not strictly geographical. They include broad areas and appeal by denomination. Their parishioners consequently have no stake in the immediate area undergoing change except insofar as it affects the church property. They are not so likely to have as rapid a turnover as the Catholic Church.

Nor are the Protestant Churches — or their ministers — wedded to a particular area, as is the Catholic Church. Very often when change takes place, the

Protestant Church follows its parishioners; it may on occasion simply close up shop, or merge with another Church, or move. The ministers, too, are in a freer position to move if there is a drastic falloff in membership — perhaps out of economic reasons. A married Protestant minister, with wife and family, faces a few more social and psychological reasons for leaving an area fast changing to all-Negro. As a family man, he is subject to somewhat the same problems and social pressures as any White family man in the community. Finally, the Protestant Church may not be as open to new members — on principle — as the Catholic Church for the simple reason that Protestant Churches tend to be organized along segregated lines. There are Negro Baptist Churches, for example, which will move into a changing area and appeal to Negroes, simply because the Baptist Church is set up along distinct lines — for Whites and for Negroes. At least in principle, the Catholic Church would never be so established.

My point is that either the Protestant Church and its minister will abandon the changing neighborhood, or a more progressive-minded minister will take on the assignment as a challenge and set to work missionizing among the new residents; a very difficult task, I might add, for a denomination that has few members or resources to start with and also is not as well staffed as the Catholic Church, for example. Regardless, the Protestant Churches are faced with adaptations in face of change just as surely as the

Catholics if they hope to win new converts. It is interesting, to say the very least, to watch the Protestant and Catholic Churches, which previously had been somewhat snug and comfortable in an all-White area, become missionary and begin to compete with one another for the new religious market in a kind of struggle for survival.

Undoubtedly the Holy Spirit has a finger in all these workings of salvation and has used racial change as a means of awakening the churches from their understandable complacency and stirring up in them a missionary zeal for new converts. Traditionally, it has been difficult enough to create much zeal for additional members in an area dominated by one religious denomination or another. Members of the dominant church feel everything is just fine because of the great number of members, and the ministers or priests usually have more than they can do to service this large membership without expending much time or effort on new frontiers.

Within the Catholic Church, we often observe more of a missionary, convert-making zeal in the South, where the Church is a small minority, than in huge urban centers with large Catholic populations. In my own experience I have seen more enthusiasm for the Confraternity of Christian Doctrine in areas where Catholics are in the minority than in areas where they are numerically strongest.

In our own community, we had to ask the question: Where does the Church make its beginning in appealing to the newcomers in the community? It is fairly evident that most efforts aimed at holding the old parishioners in the community are doomed to failure unless supported by the community at large. Religious reasons, such as parish loyalty, are far down on the list of considerations the people make when they decide to move from one area to another. Economic, social, racial, and others all come first. It is the rare Catholic who says he intends to stay in a particular neighborhood regardless of change so that he can help his priests in their missionary work among the newcomers — although such commitment is perhaps one of the highest forms of missionary work a Catholic could participate in. While such a commitment cannot be expected from many parishioners, I firmly believe a small number of parishioners, perhaps single people and young married couples, should make a firm decision not to flee in face of change but to stay on at least for several years simply and solely to put themselves at the disposal of their priests and at the disposal of their community leaders out of a genuine missionary calling.

Somehow these people will keep the Christian ideal alive and be a sign of contradiction to those who panic and run. The urban problem today cries out for this kind of Christian witness. It calls out for Christians who will voluntarily try to live the Christian ideal of brotherhood, of love and fraternal charity, even in face of hardship, ridicule, and at the sacrifice of perhaps a nicer home in a nicer neighborhood or in a so-called status neighborhood. The new parish taking shape as well as the new community needs leadership during its critical periods of transition. It needs continuity of leadership until new leaders can be raised up to carry on the work of Church and community. The priests need the support of the most loyal parishioners in this time of change.

I am not speaking glibly of this matter, for in St. Francis de Paula parish a small, hard-core group of parishioners have made just such commitments. For the most part formed in the lay apostolate through the Young Christian Workers and the Christian Family Movement, these young apostles — single and married — number about six young couples and several single people. Some of these young couples were products of the YCW in St. Francis de Paula two and three years ago before change took place; others moved by choice into St. Francis de Paula parish because of the challenge it presented and because a community of such like-minded people slowly was developing. These young people, married and single, staff the CCD high school of religion program in the parish; they do the home-visiting in the convert-making program; they are active in the Christian Family Movement and the Holy Name Society; they are giving leadership to the participation of the people in the liturgy; and beyond the parish they are giving leadership to several community associations, namely, the West Avalon Community Association, the North Avalon Community Association and even to the supra-organization on the southeast — the South East Community Organization. Here is an example of what a group of fifteen well-trained lay apostles can do in a changing neighborhood both at parish and community level. Such a group is an invaluable asset to the pastor and his priests, without which their task would almost be hopeless. In an age when there is much talk about the Papal Volunteers and the Peace Corps, these young people might be pioneering what someday will be known as a Parish Corps.

When the present pastor of St. Francis de Paula was assigned to an already fast-changing parish, one of the first projects he undertook was a parish census. Late in 1959 he initiated a series of regular meetings between himself, his curates and several lay leaders to plan for the first time in the history of the parish a parish census. Despite the fact that the parish already was in the throes of flux — people continually moving in and out — the group felt a parish census was essential to inform the priests on the current state of the parish.

As the meetings progressed, the plan of the census took shape. It was scheduled for spring, 1960. It would take the form of a so-called flash census, with the goal of completing it within a two-week span. The census would canvass every residence within the parish boundaries. The census card itself would be thorough in giving detailed information.

Looking back on the project, the critical question was whether or not we felt enough manpower could be mustered to undertake such an extensive canvass, especially in face of the fact of a steadily dwindling number of so-called pillars of the parish, most of whom already had moved away. Once extensive maps of the neighborhood were prepared (with the help of grammar-school boys, every street number was charted), the parish was divided into 175 zones of some thirty calls to a zone, which gave us some three thousand residences, apartment or home, to call upon within a two-week period. The plan was to recruit census workers, preferably in teams, for each zone. The manpower problem was quite sizeable.

Nonetheless the committee pushed ahead with its plans. Census cards were obtained, a four-page brochure about St. Francis de Paula parish was prepared and printed for mass distribution, worksheets were prepared for each zone, and target dates were set. The priests began to preach on the approaching census to enlist an all-parish cooperative effort at making it go smoothly and on schedule. Easter Sunday was established as the first date. Since most of the parishioners could be expected at church on Easter Sunday, it was decided to pass out census cards to everyone at the Easter Masses, have them completed and returned to the rectory by mail or in the collection basket within a week or two. This would eliminate most of the Catholics from the house-to-house calls and cut down on the manpower needs. As a matter of record, we received excellent cooperation from the parishioners on this part of the census.

Target dates were set for phase two, the actual canvass, which was to be on two successive Sunday afternoons. There would be a first canvass and then a kind of cleanup canvass and pickup program on the following Sunday. It was set for May. To recruit manpower for this part of the program, the committee embarked on a bold recruitment scheme. Rather than leave the matter up to pulpit requests for volunteers — voted most unlikely to yield the number of workers actually needed — we decided to canvass all parish organizations for lists of their able-bodied workers. We compiled a list of some 150 so-called active men and women, young adults, and even a few teenagers.

Once the list was completed, the pastor simply wrote every person on it a letter in which he assigned him to work a zone in the census on such and such a date between such and such hours. The assignment was specific. The letter stressed that only a several-hour commitment was being expected, certainly a small sacrifice, and that the pastor was counting on this person to do the job, or else phone him personally, if unable, so he could find a substitute. The calculated risk was that the people would respond to a direct appeal by the pastor.

It was a good risk. The people responded. Except in cases of illness or prior commitments to be out of town, the men and women contacted took the assignment in stride. More than one hundred recruits were signed up by this method. To complement this group of parishioners, the Young Christian Workers of St. Francis de Paula made a drive for volunteers from among YCWers on Chicago's South Side. Another twenty-five workers came out from this appeal. Finally, fifty seminarians were recruited from Quigley preparatory seminary and the Maryknoll seminary in Glen Ellyn, Illinois. The Maryknollers came on a weekday to help with the cleanup program and cover the few remaining areas. In all, 175 census workers were in action during the two-week period. By June 1, the entire census was complete. Many of the workers worked two and three zones to help get the job done on schedule. It was a gratifying experience for the whole parish.

Apart from contacting every residence in the parish boundaries and thus finding out where the Catholics of the parish were located, the census produced many side-benefits. Some 150 people expressed some kind of interest in the Catholic Church, a list we were able to follow up on last fall when we had a drive for our fall Inquiry Class. Most of the people in the neighborhood accepted the brochure on the parish, which informed them about the church, services, parish organizations, priests, school facilities, the Sisters of St. Francis, and exact information on where the school and church were located. This served as a general introduction of the parish to newcomers in the area.

From the point of view of the census-workers, I personally believe the experience was beneficial to them in many ways. Not only was it an experience in Catholic Action, in participation in the missionary work of the Church, but for most of them this was a first opportunity to make personal contact with the Negro in our neighborhood and to visit his home. I am sure this was an eye-opening experience for most of the people, and from what I was able to hear, it was gratifying. Again and again we heard the remark that the Negroes were much more friendly and receptive than the Whites. Only a few grumbled about the fact of being assigned to all-Negro buildings or asked for all-White zones to work in.

The entire census project turned into an all-parish effort and perhaps the first such effort in our parish to engage a great many people in an apostolic venture. Even the presence of seminarians on the scene for one day and the ability to join their efforts to those of the teenagers in our parish had many fine benefits. The relationship between seminarian and teenager was healthy; it gave our teenagers a chance to mingle and work with average-guy seminarians and see dedication in the flesh. A barbecue and softball game built into the day's activities created a good feeling among the youth. Three of our teenagers were fascinated enough in Maryknoll to make a trip out to visit the seminary.

The information gathered on the census cards has helped the parish launch some realistic programs. Names and addresses of all grammar and high school students attending public schools taken from the census cards have given us an accurate contact list for the parish Confraternity of Christian Doctrine classes.

Some thirty public high school students, mostly newcomers, are now enrolled in a Sunday morning high school of religion program.

The priests have discovered that nearly three hundred senior citizens live in our parish, many of whom need all kinds of services. The Holy Name Society is establishing committees to help these people. Priests have gotten leads on marriage cases and many other kinds of religious problems to follow up. Admittedly, the parish has been undergoing continual change since the census, but nonetheless enough information was gathered at the time to give a realistic picture of some of the parish problems. The next census will not be as difficult, and the priests are hopeful of building on what has been so far discovered. Census cards are continually being distributed to new parishioners as they come into the parish.

Besides the parish census, some beginnings in participation in the liturgy had been undertaken in 1960 in the form of dialogue Masses for adults and children, sung Masses for the children, increased participation in the Holy Week liturgy. Four laymen take turns leading the parish in a Sunday dialogue Mass from the front pew and with aid of the microphone. Besides leading the congregation in responses to the celebrant, the lay leaders say the Collect, Epistle, Gospel, and Postcommunion prayer in English. Other liturgical reforms are at the planning stage.

Whereas the Young Christian Workers group was disbanded for lack of young adults (the Whites have mostly moved; the parish does not yet know the new-comers well enough), the Christian Family Movement has grown and has broken the color line. Integrating the CFM was a pioneer step that has been exceptionally successful to date. Currently the CFM shows one integrated group, one newly formed group of young married couples, and a program for couples having taken instructions but not yet received into the Church. Finally, the parish Young Christian Students is still struggling along among a small minority of White teenagers left in the parish, sort of lost souls amidst a Negro teenage majority. Hopefully, YCS will soon be integrated and YCW will be started again.

In the summer of 1960, it was the good fortune of the parish that a priest with some fifteen years experience in changing parishes and Negro convert work was assigned to St. Francis de Paula to help launch the missionary program among the newcomers. Under the direction of the new curate, a convert-winning campaign was successfully launched in the parish in the fall of 1960.

Organizing a committee of some ten laymen as a task-force to visit homes and follow up potential candidates for instructions, the parish made a broad-side mailing into every home in the neighborhood. The mailing informed the residents about the parish and also announced dates for a convert class. A business reply card was enclosed to facilitate the response of all those interested. Returns from this mailing plus the 150 names of interested people uncovered during the parish census plus the parents of non-Catholic children now being admitted to our grammar school, became the working list for the home visitors. These men went door to door in teams to contact people and extend to them a personal invitation to attend the instruction course.

Approximately 150 people enrolled in the first series of twenty-six instructions in the fall of 1960. Classes were offered mornings and evenings twice weekly for thirteen weeks in order to accommodate the work schedules of everyone interested. Of the 150 some 85 persevered with the course to its completion; some 40 per cent were delayed or disqualified for entrance into the Church because of insoluble marriage problems; twenty actually were baptized, with another fifteen or twenty expected to come into the Church at a later date. Two of the parish priests worked together in giving the instructions. In addition to the class instructions, private interviews were held two and three times with each candidate.

Immediately after Christmas, another series of instructions was begun. Again the home-visiting teams did the personal contact work and some sixty-five registered for the winter course, which was concluded by Easter Sunday. In later courses the priests rely heavily on the previous candidates to supply names of friends or relatives who might be interested. After Easter a third course was offered, as the schedule is set up on a three times a year basis. Little by little momentum is being increased. In some all-Negro parishes in Chicago as high as three hundred converts are made each year. We counted eighty from our efforts last year.

In the considered judgment of the priests of St. Francis de Paula, the residents of our community are ripe for reception into the Catholic Church. No Protestant Church of any comparable size exists in the area nor is there any serious effort being made by the Protestants to reach the newcomer, largely because of lack of resources and staff. The priests feel that whereas most of the Negro women may be religiously committed, not so the men. Hence, the appeal is to the men, particularly younger family men, on the conviction that when a young couple has children of school age, the parents are most susceptible to a religious appeal. If ever the parents are to think about affiliating with a Church, it would be at the vulnerable period when their children start to school.

Over and above these religious motivations, there are some sociological factors which operate in favor of the Catholic Church in our type of middle-class neighborhood. I believe the Negro people are anxious to affiliate with what they probably think of as a middle-class Church in contradistinction to storefront Churches, for example, which the poorer class Negroes have traditionally joined. The Catholic Church has stature and status, it has a wonderful school system (private, not public), it has the dedicated religious Sisters, whom the Negroes respect as teachers and as a good influence on their children, it has a more rational and less emotional appeal than the stomp-and-shout storefront religion. In their efforts to disassociate themselves in this new neighborhood from all the symbols of the old, overcrowded, slum-like ghetto, the Negroes are attracted to the Catholic Church and to a certain status among White people which this entails.

At the moment I am not debating the merits of these reasons for becoming Catholic, I am simply describing situations which lead these people to present themselves for instructions. Whether or not they are given the gift of faith and are eventually accepted for Baptism is another matter and is up to the discretion of the Holy Spirit. If it were not for the fact that many of these people are disqualified from membership in the Church because of previous marriage difficulties, I feel quite sure there would be a large-scale movement of Negroes into the Catholic Church. Most of them now know that divorce is an impediment to becoming a Catholic and accordingly eliminate themselves from consideration for candidacy.

As it is, the Catholic Church has a wonderful opportunity to convert many Negroes as they become more educated, more secure in their job opportunities and more equal in the housing market, and as they throw off their heritage of Southern repression. The emotional kind of religion, and all its cult characteristics bred in the ghetto, will fade out as the Negro is able to integrate into American society and take his place alongside his White neighbor in job and community. Perhaps segregated Protestant sects (along with the new brand of Negro Mohammedanism and its Black Supremacy principle) will disappear, too. These are products of our own White discrimination. They breed in ghettos and will continue to breed so long as we fail to open our neighborhoods, our Churches, our places of employment, our schools, and our business establishments to our Negro brothers.

Once Negroes become members of the Catholic Church — whether as Catholics just moved into a new parish, or as recent converts — the problem of integrating them into the Catholic life of the parish remains, particularly if the White parishioners are still in a clear majority in the parish. When the ratio is lop-sided in favor of one group over another, psychologically speaking the minority group will find it difficult to develop a parish spirit, to feel a sense of belonging, and to feel genuinely accepted.

Steps need to be taken to bring the new parishioners into existing parish organizations, to activate them in the parish, to bring them into contact and friendship with longstanding parishioners. In the case of recent converts there is the added problem of not abandoning them in the large parish structure once they are baptized and allowing them to drift and shift for themselves. They need to feel like members of their new Church; they need to feel accepted, welcomed, wanted, appreciated; they need a sense of participation both in the worship life and in the apostolic life of the parish; and above all, they need a continued deepening of thier understanding of the newly acquired truths of the faith, either through discussion groups, reading, refresher courses, adult education, participation in study-action groups (such as CFM, YCW, or CCD discussion groups). We tend to underestimate the tremendous zeal these new Catholics have after Baptism, their enthusiasm, their desire to work to bring others into the Church. It is a zeal that puts the faith of born Catholics to shame. All of this good will and enthusiasm dare not be lost or dissipated. Followup programs need to be developed.

The priests of our parish believe that the mass organizations, such as the Holy Name Society, need development during this period of racial change. Within a mass organization, the members feel a part of something big and going. They can participate in Communion Masses, processions, breakfasts, and other general activities that bring members together. Also, within a mass organization many committees and services and projects can be set up in which almost every man can be involved. All this gives these men a sense of identity, loyalty, belonging. This is very important to their psychological well-being within the Church. The new converts likewise can be put to work at once in home-visiting and followup work for the forthcoming convert instruction series and also for the CCD schools of religion. They sincerely want to become a part of this work and take joy in it. We have found, too, that those couples who take instructions but for some reason or another still have doubts

99

and still hesitate to take the final step of Baptism are ripe for discussion-action groups, such as CFM, to keep them in touch, keep them thinking about the Church and stimulated, with the hope that whatever doubts they have can be resolved in good time.

Oftentimes, the kind of lowest common denominator approach that is taken in a large instruction class may be the only practical way to teach a diversified group, but it runs the risk of not satisfying the more serious-minded, questioning, intellectual type of candidate. He is not satisfied with simple answers but wants to go deeper and more personally into matters theological.. CCD discussion groups or CFM groups can help this person cross the threshold into the Catholic Church.

Gradually, integration will come about in the parish, first of all in the church itself at worship and at the communion rail, then in parish activities and parish organizations, at Communion breakfasts, picnics, parent-teacher meetings, school athletic banquets, and finally in homes, in group discussion work or other kinds of Catholic Action meetings, perhaps even socially at a card party or coffee klatch. One by one the barriers of race and color of skin will break down as the Mystical Body of Christ begins anew to live a healthy life in the parish. From this point of view, the Church, whether Protestant or Catholic, becomes one of the most important institutions in the community in levelling barriers, easing tensions, and contributing to community spirit.

As one of the largest and most stable institutions in the urban neighborhood, the Catholic Church (this applies to other denominations, too) must look outward to the community in which it lives. It must keep strong lines of communication with community associations and all the other institutions in the community so that it can make its contribution to the birth of a new and stable community growing out of the wreckage of quick racial turnover. The leadership the Church gives its own people in terms of community responsibility often will be the decisive factor in any community crisis, for whether anyone likes it or not, politically speaking the Catholic Church is the key power group in the community. The Church, through her priests and lay leaders, must be very conscious of how it uses this favored position to work for a better, healthier community. In a community situation where race becomes an issue, for example, the Church must articulate the Christian attitude in the community and educate its own people in that attitude.

In the United States, the local neighborhood community in which the parish finds itself is vital and is something in which average citizens — whether in block clubs or in supra-community organizations — are deeply interested. I would go so far as to say that these neighborhood associations are a democratic safeguard against complete absorption of the individual in the large and complex organizations which mark our society today, whether in economic life, labor, politics, government, and even religion.

The basic American problem today of man being lost in large collectivities was nowhere better pinpointed than in the 1960 annual statement of the American hierarchy, entitled "The Need for Personal Responsibility." The bishops said:

> Although personal responsibility and initiative have been our national characteristics, explaining in large measure our country's progress in human welfare, yet pressures are growing for a constantly greater reliance on the collectivity rather than on the individual. An inordinate demand for benefits, most easily secured by pressures of organization, has led an ever growing number of our people to relinquish their rights and to abdicate their responsibilities. This concession creates a widening spiral of increasing demands and pressures with a further infringement of increasing demands and responsibility.

I sincerely believe that citizens themselves, by grouping together in all kinds of voluntary community associations, are expressing their own reaction to the "organization age" and are taking matters again into their own hands as an expression of personal responsibility in the neighborhood-community framework. These associations are becoming the buffer groups between the lonely individual and the large, anonymous collectivity.

If we accept the fact that in the United States the neighborhood community is a vital force in urban centers — especially, given our family-centered rather than work-centered culture — then we must carefully examine the relationship of the parish to the

nmunity. Certainly, everyone will agree that
not superimpose the parish on the neighbor-
community and fuse the two into one community
interests and goals. This may have been possible
rural areas in the past, or even in the city in those
ast-disappearing ethnic parishes which were formed
by immigrants. But not so today.

Neither can we look upon the parish as just another
voluntary association within the community, existing
alongside a community association. The parish did
not come into existence out of a recognition of some
community need. It came into existence through the
waters of Baptism. It is a community of faith, completely disassociated from any community needs. In
the eyes of faith, it is self-enclosed.

Granting all this, we must still view the parish as
an institution which exists in a given neighborhood
community, just as a bank, a community association,
schools, parks, shopping areas, exist there. It is this
network of institutions which make up the community
and in some way or another serve or fail to serve the
needs of the people. The parish in this sense partici-
pates in the pluralistic society of the neighborhood
community. It cannot impose its will upon the other
institutions in the community — even though in most
cases the Catholic Church in an urban neighborhood
is the largest, most powerful, institution in the community. It cannot become a pressure group.

Those, therefore, who suggest that priests should
act more as counsellors than as directors in community

affairs sense the danger of clericalism in community action. The neighborhood community is a segment of the temporal order, where the layman, having the greatest stake in these efforts for stable communities, has first claim and must take the initiative and give the leadership.

We find this idea beautifully supported in the Bishops' statement on personal responsibility: "The response belongs to the individual person, as our Holy Father indicated: 'Fully conscious of what is at stake, moved by apostolic zeal, he then makes a personal engagement with those communities that surround him, the result of a free and justified choice of careful thought about himself, his destiny and the world.'" (Letter of July 12, 1960, to "Semain Sociale" in Grenoble.)

To quote further from the Bishops on what personal responsibility is in the context of man's relation to the world: "It presupposes the acceptance of one's dignity as a son of God in whatever environment he may be placed and the acknowledgment of binding moral law. It requires the free and deliberate acceptance of one's obligations in the position he occupies — in the family, in the Church, in the corporation, in the labor union, in the community, in the nation, in the family of nations. It demands the rule of conscience, not self-satisfaction."

This last statement is the key principle which should guide the parish in its relationship to the community. The parish has the primary role of forming the conscience of its parishioners. In describing the function of the Church, Pius XII (quoted by the Bishops) said: "Always and everywhere, by unceasingly adapting herself to the circumstances of time and place, she seeks to model persons, individuals and, as far as possible, all individuals according to the laws of Christ, thus attaining the moral basis for social life. The object of the Church is man, naturally good, imbued, enobled and strengthened by the truth and grace of Christ." If our priests would meditate on these words, they would find the answer to the role of the Church in community affairs.

It is my belief that the specialized movements of Catholic Action are the agencies within the parish that can best attain this end of modelling persons according to the laws of Christ and thus attaining the moral basis for social life which Pius XII spoke about. The Christian Family Movement in particular and the Young Christian Workers, as a matter of record, have given to the city of Chicago an extraordinarily large number of community leaders.

It would make an interesting sociological study to look into the many voluntary community associations within Chicago to discover how many of the key leaders have come up through the apostolic ranks of the Christian Family Movement, Cana, and the Young Christian Workers. I can think of ten such leaders in my own parish. This is the quiet revolution that is taking place in the Archdiocese of Chicago.

This is as it should be — the Church acting in the

temporal order through apostolically-formed lay men and women, not politically through priest-representatives of the large, monolithic and vested institution of the Church. All the good intentions in the world will not lessen the suspicion in the public eye that the priest is acting to protect the interests of the Church. Whenever the Church places herself in such a politically suspect position — whether in regard to federal aid to education or in local community affairs — the image of the Church suffers in our pluralistic American society and Catholic-Protestant relations are damaged.

I do not believe there is anything the enlightened Catholic layman resents more than to see his Church, with all its massive resources, power, finances, and organizational machinery, move into a local community or political situation as a power group. Even with all the best motives in the world — even for the salvation of souls — this mobilization of the Church behind a temporal objective is shocking and, from all theological principles, inconsistent with the nature of the Church. How can there be a sense of personal responsibility on the part of the Christian within such a framework? In saying this, I am not being anticlerical. I am merely saying what our Bishops have said: such action is outside the function of religion.

Whatever valid arguments one may make against rapidly changing neighborhoods, one good effect has been that the problems raised have brought priests and ministers out of their rectories and into the stream of community life. In solid and stable communities, where little change or transition has taken place, the priests or ministers of the large denominations in the community have seldom been challenged to community-consciousness. If anything, they have been used as kind of window-dressing for community activities, giving pious invocations at public functions.

What a change takes place in a community in transition and crisis, however, as priest and minister dig into the practical, everyday problems of maintaining and developing a stable community. Rather than meet each other perfunctorily, Catholic and Protestant and Jewish churchmen now roll up their sleeves together in meetings with community leaders in give-and-take discussion and collaboration at the very practical level of community action. This is a wonderful thing to behold; it might be called a kind of first step at an ecumenical effort between religious denominations at the neighborhood level. I have sat in on some wonderful sessions of this kind which can do nothing but bring about a better understanding and fraternity among priests and ministers.

In summary, it seems to me that the Church in a changing community has a threefold mission. First of all, it can and must develop a worshipping community among the faithful. Participation of the people in the liturgy must become the primary concern of the parish, not only for the sake of religious solidarity among the faithful, but because a worshipping community will be a powerful witness in the community at large and will attract newcomers. The parish that prays together will stay together.

Secondly, the parish must engage in a missionary effort to win converts to the faith among the newcomers and then integrate these newcomers into the life of the parish.

Thirdly, the parish must train, form, encourage, and infuse with apostolic zeal a goodly number of its leaders to go forth into the neighborhood community and give leadership in building up and maintaining a stable, healthy community life. These lay leaders will participate fully in the community, not as representatives of the Church, but as Christians, as citizens, as men and women with a stake in the community but who have a deep sense of personal responsibility, as Christians, to their fellow men.

Sustained by their priests, full of the graces brought to them through a vital worshipping community, they will indeed represent Christ at the community level.

This I take to be an exact statement of the role of the Church in the community.

LONELINESS AMIDST CHANGE

It is difficult enough trying to finalize some thoughts on any subject let alone the question of changing neighborhoods. *Revolution in the City* has been three years in the making — if only three months in the writing. Now, as the time is at hand to draw the book to a conclusion, I fully realize that already new changes are taking place in our South Side Chicago community, changes about which I find I cannot at this time make any final statements. The reader of this small work will need to bear in mind that what he reads was so at the time of writing and may not be so at the time of reading. Life goes on in our fast-changing community, and stability still is in the far distance. While there are no doubt many communities — even in the big cities — that one could write a book about and be certain that, fifteen or even twenty years from now, the book would still be basically true, not so a community such as ours, to which each day brings new surprises and challenges.

In these final pages of *Revolution in the City*, I want to strike a personal note by giving my own impressions of living in a community that has changed from all-White to almost all-Negro. I want to give these impressions to reassure everyone that I do not consider myself some kind of hero or martyr or social reformer or bug-eyed liberal or flag-waving civil rightist because I have made an attempt at living in a racially mixed community. On the one hand, I neither want nor expect Brotherhood medals to be pinned on me for such a commitment, but on the other hand, I do want to share with my readers the experience I have had, to take you behind the scenes of my own life in a community that now finds the few remaining White people in the small minority role — a completely reversed role with the Negro, who only three years ago constituted the minority group. What is it like to live through this reversal of roles?

At this writing I look up and down the block I live in to survey its present state. In a rough estimate, some 60 per cent of the single-family units on the block are now owned by Negroes; the remaining 40 per cent by White people. Because our block is perhaps the only block in the community that has no apartment buildings in it, no doubt the White-Negro ratio is not representative of the community. In the apartment areas, the ratio is more like 90 to 95 per cent Negro to 5 to 10 per cent White. At this moment, however, I am looking at my own block.

What has it been like to live now some three years on a block that is racially mixed? More specifically, what is it like to live next door to Negroes? I phrase this last question, because this seems to be the issue that is uppermost in the minds of White people. Work next to Negroes, yes; be friendly with them, yes; but live next door to them, never. This pretty well sums up the attitude of White people in Chicago. Unlike in the South, where White people are not concerned with how close the Negro gets to him, so long as he doesn't get higher, in the North, the White man does not care how high the Negro gets, just so he doesn't get close to him. That seems to be one of the major differences between the racial problem in the North and in the South.

I have no compunction in admitting that the Negro family living next door to me — from all outward appearances — fits the stereotype of the kind of Negro family white people are repulsed by — large family, from the South, no formal education, a very modest, overcrowded home in need of repairs. I admit to all these things for the simple reason that none of this in real life is as frightening as it is in stereotyped life. As a matter of fact, my neighbor is a good neighbor, a friendly, peaceful, reliable, stable, hard-working family man, with a loyal, loving wife who also is a very good mother.

When friends tell me how much my status has been lowered by living next door to such a family (they are quick to cite my college degrees — something which I would like to forget), I simply ask them if they have stopped to consider how much I have raised my neighbor's status. When they ask me if I am going to paint my house, I answer (facetiously, of course) that I am not, because I don't want to get ahead of my neighbors, I want to maintain the neighborhood standards.

So, there are seven kids living next door to me. With all that, I didn't find more or less kids climbing my cherry tree this summer than I did in the past. Color has nothing to do with a child's insatiable desire for red cherries at the top of the tree. What I am trying to say in all this is that in my block life goes on the same as usual — no worse or better than before the Negroes moved in. Not being the type that ever took delight in visiting back and forth with my neighbors, I am neither more nor less sociable than I ever was. We have our over-the-fence discussions; we are friends; we trust one another; help one another. I don't believe most Americans expect much more than this from their neighbors. The suburban "togetherness" never did quite prevail in the inner cities.

When I look up and down my street today, the block actually seems to be in good shape. Five new brick homes have been built on it in the past several years; quite a few of the frame homes have been painted or sided. Everyone is out puttering with their lawns. About the only real change I have observed has been cultural. I first noticed it this past Memorial Day. I believe every backyard on the block — and that includes mine — was the site for an outdoor barbecue. A black cloud literally hung over the neighborhood. I understand barbecues are quite common in the suburbs, too; but I had never noticed them so widespread in our neighborhood before.

Unless you are allergic to barbecue smoke, I really don't see any problems in living in an integrated block, or in living next door to Negroes. Until White Americans get some of these bugaboos out of their system — including the phony problem of status — I really don't believe we are going to make much progress with the racial problem in the United States. At least in the big urban centers, the matter is going to come down to a question of living next door to Negroes — of living in integrated communities. We simply cannot go on in the pattern of panic flight from the problem. Open occupancy will come, sooner or later, and the more we work to bring it about by peaceful and legal means the less racial militancy we will have on the part of the Negro.

In my own humble estimation, the real heroes in the struggle for integration are not so much the demonstrators who participate in dramatic civil rights activities, as the quiet, simple people who are making a living lie out of housing segregation in their day to day round of family activities in integrated neighborhoods. There is no fanfare here, no publicity, no propaganda, no militancy, just a simple coming to grips with the basic problem in a very human, personal way. There is no substitute for this approach. It is free of politics, pressure groups, agencies, national organizations, antagonisms, violence, hatreds. It is free, voluntary, natural, in life, and personal.

So much for interracial living on my block. If life on my block were representative of life in my community, I would have no problems at all. Unfortunately, life is not that simple. I would be less than honest if I did not confess to you at this writing that a terrible loneliness has overcome me in the Grand Crossing-West Avalon community on the South Side of Chicago. The loneliness is not so much a block problem as it is a community problem. I think I can talk about this loneliness now in a way that both White and Negro will understand it. As a member of a small White remnant in our neighborhood, which is now fast becoming all-Negro, I am beginning to experience something the Negro must experience when he finds himself alone in an all-White society. I am happy for the experience, although not happy with the gnawing loneliness.

Perhaps I would not feel this loneliness had I not been such an intimate part of the White community that fled when the Negro began to move in. This was not just a community in which I happened to live. It was one I chose to live and work in. It was one that I spent a great deal of time sinking roots into, developing personal relationships and friendships in, involving myself at both the community and the Church level. In this sense, I now share my loneliness with the White people who moved out (I know how they must have felt when they pulled stakes and started life over again in a new community) and I share it with the Negroes who have so often found themselves alone in a dominantly White society. In this community which has moved out from under me to be replaced by a community I can't quite feel at home in, either psychologically or even spiritually,

114

I find myself in a unique position of feeling empathy with both sides. I feel the human problems and up- heavals both Whites and Negroes have gone through in the big city.

But let us look at the problem of loneliness. I re- member back one and two summers when I would walk over to Grand Crossing park in the evening. Without exaggeration, I could walk through that park and identify two hundred young people by name — as they played softball or swam in the pool, and they knew my name. This was not due to any kind of photographic memory on my part, but I knew these young people in a personal way. I had nurtured con- tacts with them in the community and through various youth programs at St. Francis de Paula Catholic Church. Some I knew more intimately than others, because we were involved in those days with at least fifty youths in intensive leadership training programs of the Young Christian Workers and Young Christian Students. Some we knew through the Friday night teen socials we sponsored, which always attracted 150 or so young people. Some we knew through the religious instruction program of the CCD for public high school students. Some we knew through coopera- tion with the park in sponsoring ball leagues. But knowing the young people of the community — this was one accomplishment we were proud of. And not only that, in many instances we knew the parents of these young people; we had worked with older brothers and sisters in years past. There was continuity and

115

tradition developing here in youth work.

This summer I would walk over to the park in the evening and recognize not one face, know not one name, have not one personal contact. What a tremendous change in two years, not only in the complete turnover — and thus the complete interruption of a tradition and destruction of a continuity that took years to nurture — but even more psychologically difficult, there was not a White teenager in the park any longer. All had either moved out of the community or changed their base of operation for athletics. I think you can understand the loneliness I experienced in Grand Crossing park this summer.

This is not to say that we cannot begin to rebuild, to start our youth work all over, begin anew to know people, learn names — and faces — cultivate associations, find entree into the homes, begin again to develop youth programs, and so on. I am not denying that all this is possible and must be done. It is part of the commitment to stay in a changing community. But having said this does not take away one bit from the heartbreak and sadness that overwhelms someone when he has had this experience. That is the only point I want to make at this time. I now know something of what it must mean to be a displaced person, a refugee, an immigrant, a member of a minority group.

There was more to developing a youth program in a community than walking through the park on a summer evening. A very important part of my own personal work in this area was to use my house as a youth center, where teenage boys could feel free to come and go for meetings or plain recreation. My home was an integral part of our youth programs. But today, all that has changed. Only a few of the boys — long since moved out — return for visits, and even they become more reluctant to come into this strange neighborhood which was once their home. More than once on their way home at night they have gotten into scrapes with Negro kids. Just as the Negro teenagers were afraid to come into this all-White neighborhood several years back, now the White kids have the same fears when entering an all-Negro neighborhood. All this goes to prove, I suppose, that human nature is pretty much the same everywhere. Even this is a consoling truth to call to mind at a time when everything is attributed to some sinister and insidious form of prejudice. The fact that I can observe prejudice working both ways indicates that perhaps, after all, color of skin is not the major factor, but "boys will be boys."

There has been a spiritual loneliness in the parish, too. No longer is the parish booming with activities, no longer is there a whole host of parish organizations. The fall-off in parish membership to something like one thousand has taken its toll in parish leadership and parish organizational life. Certainly it has depleted the youth resources. Newcomers to the parish, oddly enough, are still in the minority, so that they must feel this loneliness, too. The remaining white people — still the majority among the church-goers — have their loneliness, too, as all their friends and neighbors one by one move away. I can quite imagine that the priests are lonely, too, as they see their church empty out and as they readjust themselves to a new kind of pastoral program geared to reach out to the Negro.

At the community level I have experienced a terrible loneliness — and a painful kind of rejection. Not that I shouldn't have expected it, but when it comes, it comes full force. I can think back on the days when a handful of us in the all-White community fought with all our energies to make this an open neighborhood. We fought to re-tool a "keep them out" improvement association so that the newcomers to our community could come into the organization and assume their rightful roles in community leadership. It was not an easy battle to fight, and the community leaders among the Whites who stood up to be counted in the battle for the rights of the Negro were few.

Then came what I might call the delightful but perhaps too complacent months when the community organization was integrated, when Negro and White, Protestant and Catholic, sat down together to solve common community problems in what both sides felt was a satisfactory and acceptable way. There was good spirit, cooperation, a working-together in all this that comprised a very satisfactory experience.

But now that terrible loneliness has set in again, this time at the community level, for it soon became obvious that as the Negro more and more dominated the community, numerically speaking, the role of the White community leader would diminish. He came face to face again with his minority position, with the reality of a situation in which he no longer could lead or represent or even be listened to. He must decrease so that they might increase. It was a kind of a John the Baptist feeling that I personally have experienced — a preparing the way for someone else, then stepping aside, letting loose, yielding to the new forces abroad in the community.

In a large, densely populated community — with all kinds of political and economic and even religious stakes to be fought for — I should have expected that new forces would be set free in the community.

A whole new community is emerging. Not only is there a tough fight for community leadership, but there are political leaders to raise up and there are economic gains to be won. In the mad scramble — most of which it is still too early to judge — the White remnant really has very little to do or say. And when the struggles for leadership among the Negroes in our community are placed in context with the struggles for power going on at the community and political and economic and religious levels throughout the South Side of Chicago in the Negro community, one can quickly see that this is no place for a White man to cast his lot, any more than a Negro leader could have made gains in our community five or ten years ago.

Being somewhat of an idealist throughout my life — a position in which I associate myself with most liberal causes — I must admit that I was not prepared to see ambitious community and political leaders (and at times, religious leaders) clothe their ambitions and drives for power in high sounding civil rights causes and try to ride to the top on militantcy in civil rights. It takes a discerning eye to spot those who are sincerely interested in the rights of minorities and in the community as such and those who carry these same banners up the ladder of personal power and prestige. In due time, however, I think the good sense of the people recognizes those who are sincerely with them and those who are using them. But again, it is the loneliness of the White man in this situation, for if he speaks out or is critical, he can so easily be accused of not being militant, liberal, or interested in civil rights. I know, for I have experienced this form of rejection, too. And if he speaks out in defense of the rights of the new minority in his community — the White people — again he is a voice in the wilderness.

These past years have not only seen a revolution in the city but also a revolution inside people themselves. What I have been able to describe of my own personal transformation during this past year, I am sure strikes a kind of universal chord in the hearts of many — Whites and Negroes — who have confronted this kind of radical uprooting of a community, whether they be displaced persons from Europe or relocated peoples in urban neighborhoods. There is a kind of common psychological experience in all these cases.

I am not ashamed to admit that this past year was a kind of year of purification for me. It has not been easy to let loose, to give up, to yield, to cut off, to experience a kind of emptying out, to diminish, to become small and ineffective, to know humiliation, to strip down to become simply a witness, to simply be present, and to try in some feeble way to testify by continued presence that there is no escape from life, that man cannot go through life running from problems or staying one jump ahead of trouble. There comes a point where we must stand upright and face the situation in life, come what sacrifices there may.

Time and time again people put the question to me. How long can you hold out? How long will you stay? When are you going to move? Try as I may, I cannot find answers to these questions. To date my conscience won't let me leave. I can find no good reason in my own life why I should move — other than to escape the Negro, and this answer I cannot accept either on religious or patriotic grounds. Something inside me compelled me to stay with these problems — perhaps so that I could experience them and communicate my experience to others, perhaps so I could understand what takes place in the hearts and minds of both Negroes and Whites when a community is struck by upheaval, perhaps so I could stay alongside those who wanted to move but couldn't escape because of economic reasons or old age or illness, perhaps so I could stay alongside those few great souls in our community who by choice decided to stay with an integrated community to help confront one of the great problems of our times at the community and parish levels. Perhaps all these reasons in one way or another are present in this decision to stay.

How long can a man stay? Perhaps that answer will have to be worked out in terms of his effectiveness, his sense of accomplishment, his personal ability to regroup his forces and start over and build anew, and his ability to overcome loneliness and feel that there are others with whom he can confide and above all work. There are no universal, pat answers to questions like these. We know only that missionaries in foreign lands must experience pretty much the same agonies, and we know they have been able to succeed. The present situation is not too much different. The role must be viewed as a missionary one, or else it would not be bearable.

This much I believe is certain. It is no solution to the problem of integration when communities are allowed to go from all-White to all-Negro. Somewhere we must strike a balance and achieve some stable, integrated communities, where no racial or cultural or ethnic group has a one-sided grasp on a community. Any community efforts or political efforts or religious efforts or economic efforts that promote a closed society as against an open society must be fought, no matter under what high-sounding and morally clothed arguments these efforts may be presented. There are no legal or moral legs to stand on in America in any kind of struggle for a closed society — whether it be a block, a neighborhood, a ward, a town or city, or a nation. Consistency of principle demands that we fight against this, regardless of race, creed, color, or national origin.